The Bug Book

The 1981 Childcraft Annual

An annual supplement to
Childcraft—The How and Why Library

World Book—Childcraft International, Inc.

A subsidiary of The Scott & Fetzer Company

Chicago London Paris Sydney Tokyo Toronto

Acknowledgments

The publishers of *Childcraft—The How and Why Library* gratefully acknowledge the courtesy of the following publishers, agencies, authors, and organizations for permission to use copyrighted material in this volume. Full illustration acknowledgments appear on page 296.

"End-of-Summer Poem" by Rowena Bastin Bennett. Reprinted by permission of Rowena Bastin Bennett.

"A Dragon-Fly" from *Eleanor Farjeon's Poems for Children*. Originally published in *Over the Garden Wall* by Eleanor Farjeon, copyright 1933, 1961 by Eleanor Farjeon. Reprinted by permission of J.B. Lippincott, Publishers, and Harold Ober Associates Incorporated.

"Fuzzy Wuzzy, Creepy Crawly" by Lilian Schulz Vanada in *Sung Under the Silver Umbrella*. Reprinted by permission of the Association of Childhood Education International, 3615 Wisconsin Avenue, N.W., Washington, D.C. Copyright 1935 by the Association.

"The Ant Village" from *Open the Door* by Marion Edey and Dorothy Grider. Copyright 1949 by Marion Edey and Dorothy Grider. Reprinted by permission of Charles Scribner's Sons.

"The Wasp" by William Sharp. Reprinted by permission of Dodd, Mead & Company, Inc., from *Collected Poems* by William Sharp.

"Mosquito" and "Praying Mantis" from *Bugs* by Mary Ann Hoberman. Copyright © 1976 by Mary Ann Hoberman. Reprinted by permission of Viking Penguin Inc., and Russell and Volkening, Inc.

"Of a Spider" by Wilfred Thorley from *The Happy Colt* by Wilfred Thorley. Reprinted by permission of George G. Harrap & Company Limited.

Contents

Preface

Do you like stories about strange creatures that live on other planets? Many people do. Most of us like new, astounding, and strange things. Yet, most people don't know that all around them are creatures just as strange, interesting, and exciting as anything there might be on another planet! They are the tiny creatures most of us call "bugs."

You probably don't pay much attention to these tiny creatures. But most of them are actually far more interesting and unusual than many animals you'll see in a zoo! A lot of the tiny creatures are truly as weird as if they came from another planet! Some can do amazing things. And many have astounding ways of life.

These tiny animals also play a big part in our lives—bigger than most of us know. Some destroy our plants, our food and belongings, and even harm us! But some are helpful. And some are very necessary to the world. However, we usually don't know which are which. We often try to kill the very ones we should be glad to see!

This book has two purposes. One is to entertain you with tales as marvelous as any you'll find in fairy tales or science fiction stories. The other is to open your eyes to the *importance*—for good and bad—of the tiny creatures we call "bugs."

The Tiny Creatures

ladybugs

We call them "bugs"

Have you ever wanted to watch wild animals close up? Well, you can! And you don't have to go to a zoo, or to Africa, or to the rain forests of South America. Just go to your own backyard, or a place with grass, bushes, trees, and water. Believe it or not, many wild animals live very close to you.

Keep your eyes open. You will find animals that crawl like snakes when they are babies, but have wings and fly when they grow up. You'll find fierce hunters that chase their prey. You'll see other hunters that hide in wait, make clever traps, or use disguises to get their meals. You'll even find animals that build "cities," have "farms," and keep herds of other animals!

All these creatures are the animals we often call "bugs." But it's a mistake to call them all by this name. They are really different kinds of animals—each kind with its own name.

You may not have paid much attention to these tiny animals before. If not, you will be amazed to discover how strange and marvelous they truly are. They are also important. Many of these tiny creatures play a big part in our lives—even though we may not know it.

So turn the page and start to find out about the many kinds of tiny wild animals that are all around you. Learn about their ways of life and the amazing things they do. Then go out and *see* them do the things you've read about.

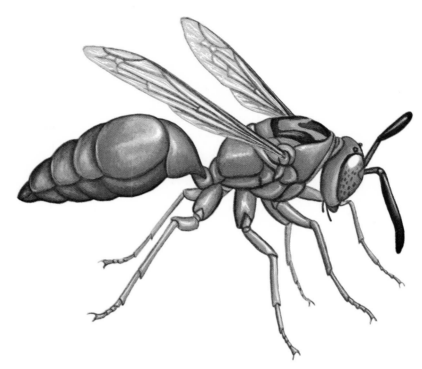

The six-legged animals

When the weather is warm, you see many tiny creatures buzzing about in the air, scurrying along the sidewalk, prowling through grass, and creeping over leaves. Most of these little creatures are the animals we call insects.

All insects have six legs. And every insect has a body with three parts—a head, a middle part, and a back part. If you touch an insect, it feels stiff and hard. This is because its body and legs are covered with hard skin. Most insects have feelers on their head. Most insects have wings, but some do not.

There are more than eight hundred thousand kinds of insects. Ants, beetles, bees, butterflies, and grasshoppers are some of the insects you see most often.

skipper butterfly

scarab beetle

green lynx spider

The eight-legged animals

Do you think a spider is an insect? Well, it's not. A spider is a very different kind of animal from an insect.

Spiders belong to the group of animals called arachnids (uh RAK nihdz). Arachnids have eight legs, while insects have only six. The body of an arachnid is divided into two parts rather than three like an insect. And no arachnid has wings or feelers.

Like insects, arachnids have a hard skin. This hard skin may cover the whole body or only a part of it. For example, a spider's legs and front part are covered with an armorlike skin. But its back part is usually rather soft.

There are more than thirty thousand kinds of spiders. And there are more than eighty thousand other kinds of arachnids. Among the best known of the other arachnids are scorpions and daddy longlegs.

Lots of legs

Sow bugs are not at all like insects or arachnids. These little creatures may have as many as twelve, fourteen, or sixteen legs. Like many insects, they have feelers. But they do not have wings.

Although they are called bugs, these tiny animals are actually crustaceans (kruhs TAY shuhnz). They belong to the same family as shrimps, lobsters, and crabs.

Most crustaceans live in salt water. Like you, they need oxygen to live. You get oxygen out of the air when you breathe. Your lungs take oxygen from the air and pass it into your blood. In this way, the oxygen gets to all parts of your body.

But crustaceans don't have lungs. Instead, they have breathing organs called gills. The gills take oxygen from water and pass it into the animals' bloodstream. Sow bugs, like most crustaceans, breathe through gills. So, even though they live on land, they have to keep wet in order to breathe.

Sow bugs, also called wood lice, are small, flat, oval-shaped creatures. They look a bit like tiny armadillos. And, like the armadillo, they curl themselves into a ball when they are disturbed. When a sow bug does this, it looks like a small, gray pill. For this reason, they are often called pill bugs.

sow bugs

Sow bugs often curl up into a ball. This helps keep them from drying out and also protects them from enemies.

Lots and lots of legs

Have you ever seen animals that look like worms with legs—lots and lots of legs? Well, they may look like worms, but they're not worms. They are animals called centipedes (SEHN tuh peedz) and millipedes (MIHL uh peedz).

Centipede means "hundred feet." But some centipedes have only thirty feet. Others have more than three hundred. *Millipede* means "thousand feet." But no millipede has this many feet. Some have as few as eight. Others have more than two hundred feet.

Centipedes and millipedes look alike, but they are really very different. Both have feelers on their head and both have a body that is divided into many sections. But a centipede has two legs—a pair—on each section of its body. A millipede has four legs—two pairs—on each section. The total number of legs each animal has depends on the number of body sections.

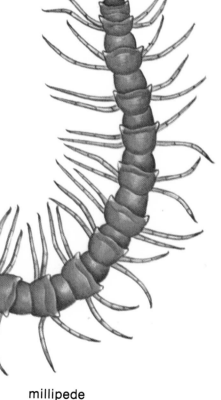

millipede

18

grasshopper

The little "fingers" near this grasshopper's mouth are its jaws. Many insects have such jaws. They work like a pair of pliers.

Plier jaws
and sipper tongues

Insects, arachnids, and other many-legged animals don't have the kind of mouth we do. Their mouth is just an open hole.

Insects have special parts around their mouth, to help them eat. The kind of mouthparts an insect has depends on the way the insect eats. Some insects, such as ants and dragonflies, chew their food. These insects have two strong jaws that stick out on each side of the mouth. These jaws work like a pair of pliers. With them, the insect tears off pieces of food, such as bits of a leaf.

The inner edges of the jaws are lined with little teeth that can grind and cut. The jaws work sideways, not up and down as yours do. If you could hear an insect chewing a bit of leaf, it would sound much like a person chewing celery!

Actually, chewing insects have two sets of jaws. Behind the chewing jaws there is another set of jaws. These jaws are somewhat like fingers. They reach out and take the chewed-up food from the front jaws. Then, the jaws curl back and push the food into the animal's mouth.

Many kinds of insects drink their food. They eat only liquids. So, their mouthparts are made for sipping. A butterfly has a long

tube that comes out of its mouth. The tube is coiled up most of the time. But when the butterfly smells nectar, the tube uncoils. Then it is a sipper, like a soda straw.

A mosquito's lower lip forms a long beak with a groove in it. Six sharp "needles" stick out from the end of the beak. The mosquito jabs the needles into the skin of an animal or person, causing blood to flow. Then it sucks up the blood through the groove in its beak. Some kinds of insects suck juice from plants in the same way.

A housefly's lower lip forms a tube with a pair of thick pads on the end. The housefly sops up liquid with the pads and sucks the liquid up into its mouth. It can also turn some things, such as sugar, into liquid, so it can eat them. To do this, it lets "spit" ooze out of its mouth onto the food. This "spit" turns the solid food into a liquid.

Spiders turn all of their food into liquid. They have a pair of curved, hollow claws just above the mouth. When they grab their prey, they shoot poison through these hollow claws. The poison turns the inside of the prey's body into a liquid. The spider then sucks in the food through a mouth tube.

Some kinds of spiders use their claws to crush their prey. Then they dissolve the prey by spraying liquid on it. The spider then sucks the food in up through its mouth tube.

alfalfa butterfly

A butterfly sips food through a long tube that comes from its mouth. Many insects have such sipping tubes.

jumping spider

A spider has fangs by its mouth. It kills its prey with the fangs.

Breathing through holes

Inside your chest is a pair of "bags" called lungs. They are much like balloons. When you breathe in, your lungs get larger. This causes them to pull in air. When you breathe out, your lungs get smaller. The air in your lungs is forced out.

An insect doesn't breathe this way. It has no lungs. An insect has a row of little holes on each side of its body. Fresh air seeps into the insect's body through the holes. The air moves about in the insect through a lot of little tubes. The "used-up" air goes back out through the holes in the insect's sides.

Caterpillars and other insects breathe through little holes in their sides.

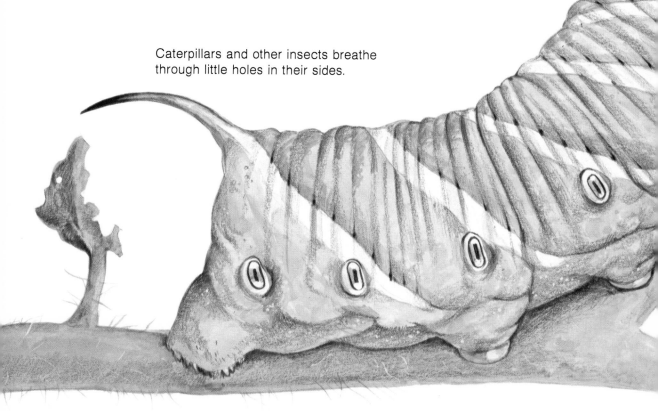

Most kinds of spiders have one pair of lungs, but some have two pairs. A spider's lungs don't work the way your lungs do. Air gets into the lungs through one or two pairs of holes on the spider's underside.

Of course, insects, spiders, and all the other many-legged animals take in fresh air for the same reason you do. They need a gas, called oxygen, that's in air. The bodies of most living creatures use oxygen as a kind of fuel. Without it, they couldn't live.

luna moth

Smelling without a nose

A luna moth skims lightly through the air on pale-green wings. It is following a smell that comes from a mile away. But the moth isn't sniffing the odor with its nose—it doesn't have a nose. It smells by means of many tiny, hairlike things on its two lacy, feathery feelers, or antennae.

Most of the many-legged animals that have feelers use them for smelling. Some kinds of insects also have "smellers" on their mouthparts. And some kinds of insects, as well as spiders, have smellers on their feet. A spider can follow a scent by walking on it!

Tasting with feet

You can't tell if something tastes good by putting your foot on it—but a fly can.

Flies, and several other kinds of insects, taste with their feet! They find good things to eat just by walking around! As a fly walks, it tastes whatever it's walking on. When it steps on something that tastes good, it stops to eat.

Other insects, such as ants and bees, taste with their feelers. When you were on a picnic, did an ant ever touch your sandwich with its feelers? It was probably trying to find out if the sandwich was good to eat.

Insects that chew their food taste with their jaws. They taste their food best when they begin to chew it, just as we do. If something doesn't taste good, the insect stops chewing and gets rid of what it was eating.

Ears in strange places

Some insects and other many-legged animals have "ears." But their "ears" aren't anything like your ears.

A katydid's ears are an opening on each of its front legs. A grasshopper has ears on each side of its body. The ears of a mosquito are like tiny hairs on its feelers. And a spider's ears are many tiny openings, like slits, in its body.

We don't really know if insects and spiders can hear all the things that we can hear. But they can hear the things that are important to them.

A spider can hear a fly that's buzzing in its web. A female katydid can hear the whirring call of a male. And many kinds of moths can hear the high-pitched squeaks made by their enemies the bats—a sound we can't hear.

katydid

A katydid has an "ear" on each of its front legs. The "ear" is an opening with a piece of thin skin stretched tight behind it.

Seeing with many eyes

Suppose, for a moment, that you could see the world through the eyes of a many-legged animal. What do you think things would look like? Certainly, they would look very different. The eyes of an insect are not like our eyes. And most spiders see things through many eyes! What can that be like?

Most insects have five eyes. Three of the eyes, which are on the insect's forehead, are very tiny and see only light. The other two eyes, which are on each side of the head, are enormous. These are the insect's main eyes.

Each main eye is made up of thousands of tiny "eyes." So, instead of seeing one whole, clear "picture" as we do, an insect probably sees things as a great many pieces that fit together to form a single picture. Thus things probably look rather blurry to an insect—like a newspaper picture when you look at it through a magnifying glass.

However, insects can probably see tiny movements better than we can. An insect's big eyes bulge out from its head. Because its eyes stick out, an insect can see ahead, on both sides, and even behind—all at the same time. It easily sees a movement anywhere around it. So it knows when something is trying to creep up on it. And hunting insects are able to find prey more easily.

People see things "whole," like the top flower. But insects probably see things in many little pieces, like the bottom flower.

damselfly

Many insects have large, round eyes that let them see in all directions at once.

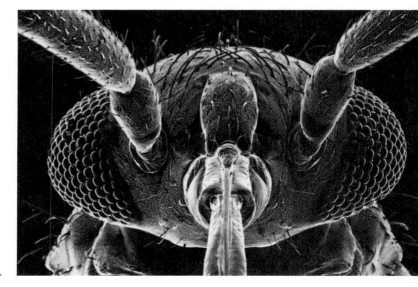

leaf bug

An insect's eyes are actually made up of many tiny eyes, as this close-up picture shows.

wolf spider

Some kinds of spiders have six eyes, like this wolf spider. Others have eight eyes.

Insects see some of the colors we see, but other colors look different to them. A bee sees yellow, blue, violet, and bluish-green. But red looks black to a bee.

However, bees see some colors we can't see. Scientists have found that some flowers have spots of color that are invisible to us. But bees and some other insects can see these colors.

A spider's eyes, however, aren't like those of an insect. A spider probably sees a whole "picture," just as we do. But most spiders have eight eyes. It is hard to imagine what things look like to a spider!

Feeling with hairs

You feel with your skin. When you touch
something, nerves in your skin tell you if
the thing is hot, cold, wet, dry, smooth,
rough, soft, hard, slick, or sticky.

An insect can't feel anything with its
hard, armorlike skin. But insects have many
tiny hairs growing out through their armor.
They use these hairs to feel all the things we
can feel. Spiders and other many-legged
creatures also have such hairs on their body.

Insects have a great many of these "touch
hairs" on their feelers. As an insect walks
about, it "explores" everything with its
feelers—touching them to everything it
comes to. With their feelers, many insects
can tell how a thing feels, smells, and
tastes—all at the same time.

So, an insect's feelers are very important.

Often, you'll see an insect bend its head and rub its feelers with its front legs. It does this to clean its feelers. It cleans them by pulling them through a special sort of "comb" on its leg. This helps keep the feelers in good working order.

Some insects can feel things we can't feel. Did you ever try to smack a fly with your hand? The fly nearly always zooms away before you can hit it. The hairs on the fly's body can feel the air moving as your hand comes down. This warns the fly to take off, at once.

Noisemakers

Insects are noisy! A fly can fill a whole room with a loud buzz as it soars and circles about. On a warm summer night, insects often keep up a steady chirp, creak, and whir. Do the noises *mean* anything? And how do the insects make these noises?

Some of the noises that insects make are not made on purpose. They just happen. The buzzing or humming sound that a flying insect makes is the sound of its wings moving very rapidly. For most insects, the sound doesn't mean anything. But for some insects, the sound the wings make is important.

The sound made by a female mosquito's wings help a male mosquito find her. A male can tell the sound of a female's wings even though there may be other noises around. By flying toward the sound, the male finds a mate.

Many of the chirps, creaks, and whirs of insects, however, are made on purpose. The insects make the noises by rubbing special parts of their bodies together, or by making a special part vibrate, or shake, rapidly.

Most of the sounds are made by male insects. They make use of some sounds to call females to them. A female goes toward the sound and finds the male. They mate, and in time she will lay eggs.

bulla

The African insect called a bulla makes "music" by scraping its legs against a row of bumps on its sides.

But some sounds mean other things. Some male crickets have special "territories" that they "own." If another male cricket comes into the territory, the owner makes a special noise that's a warning. It means "Get out or I'll fight you!"

Often, a whole group of the same kind of insects will make the same kind of noise. This is a way of calling others of their kind, both males and females, to come to them. A grasshopper that's alone will head toward noise made by a group of others of its kind. This brings many grasshoppers together so they can find mates easily.

Insects aren't the only many-legged animals that make noise. Some kinds of male spiders also have special body parts they rub together to make noise.

Growing up

Suppose you saw two flies standing close together. And suppose one fly was much smaller than the other. You would probably think the small one was a baby fly.

Actually, they would be two different kinds of flies. And both would be grown-ups. You can always tell a grown-up insect by its wings. Baby insects don't have wings. Baby insects aren't little creatures that look like their parents, as do many kinds of baby animals. Most baby insects don't look at all like their parents.

A fly begins life inside an egg. The egg looks like a grain of rice. When the egg hatches, usually in a few hours, out comes the baby fly.

The baby fly doesn't look a bit like a grown-up fly. It has no wings, no feelers, and no legs. It looks like a tiny white worm. Many kinds of baby insects look like worms. Such wormlike babies are called larvae (LAHR vee).

Larvae don't do anything but eat and grow. But their skins don't grow, as ours do. A larva (LAHR vuh) grows *inside* its skin. When the skin becomes too tight, it splits open, usually down the back. Then the larva crawls out of the old skin! It may do this several times while it is "growing up."

A time comes when the larva has eaten

enough and grown enough. Then it spins a silk covering, or forms a sort of shell around itself. Now it has become what is called a pupa (PYOO puh).

The young insect lies quietly inside its covering. Slowly, its body changes. It grows long legs and feelers. In most cases it grows wings—although some kinds of grown-up insects don't have wings. After some time it

life cycle of a butterfly

A butterfly, like many other insects, has four stages of life. It begins life as a tiny egg. When it breaks out of the shell it is a wormlike larva, or caterpillar. The caterpillar becomes a pupa. A hard shell, called a chrysalis forms around the pupa. Inside the shell, the pupa changes into an adult butterfly.

adult

egg

larva (caterpillar)

pupa (chrysalis)

grasshopper nymph

A grasshopper, like many other insects, has three stages of life. It begins as an egg. When it hatches, it looks much like an adult, but has no wings. It is called a nymph. The nymph becomes an adult without going through a pupa stage.

breaks out of its covering. Now it has a body exactly like that of its parents. It has grown up. It will never grow any bigger.

Some kinds of insect babies, such as grasshoppers, are only a little different from their parents. They have legs and feelers. But they may have shorter, stubby bodies. And at this age they don't yet have wings. This kind of insect baby is called a nymph (nihmf).

A nymph is tiny when it comes out of its egg. It, too, grows by climbing out of its skin from time to time. Each time, its body gets a little bigger and its wings grow a bit. Finally, its wings swell up to full size. Now

katydid nymph
This young katydid is pulling itself out of its old skin. All young insects grow by shedding their hard outer skin from time to time.

the insect is an adult. It will never grow any more.

Some kinds of wingless insects, as well as spiders, centipedes, and millipedes, have babies that look just like their parents. These babies, too, often molt, or shed their skin and grow a new one. Some kinds keep on growing all their lives. Even after they are adults, they shed their skin and get bigger from time to time.

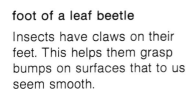

foot of a leaf beetle

Insects have claws on their feet. This helps them grasp bumps on surfaces that to us seem smooth.

Walking upside down

You'll often see a fly, spider, or other many-legged creature walk straight up a wall. And these creatures can stroll about on a ceiling as easily as you walk on the floor. They don't seem to care a bit that they're walking upside down! How can they do this without falling?

A wall or ceiling may look quite smooth to us. But for a tiny insect, it's as rough and bumpy as a road full of boulders. Each of an insect's six legs has two claws at the end. As it walks, an insect simply grabs hold of the rough bumps on a wall or ceiling with its claws. Spiders, too, have two or three claws on each of their eight legs.

Insects can also walk on very smooth surfaces, such as windows and mirrors. They can do this because they also have hairy pads on their feet. A moist, sticky substance in the pads sticks to smooth surfaces and keeps the insect from falling.

As for being upside down, this doesn't bother a spider or insect in the least. Their brains are very different from ours. For them, walking upside down probably doesn't seem any different from being right side up.

Where do they go in winter?

The little songs of summer are all gone today.
The little insect instruments are all packed away:
The bumblebee's snare drum, the grasshopper's
    guitar,
The katydid's castanets—I wonder where they are.
The bullfrog's banjo, the cricket's violin,
The dragonfly's cello have ceased their merry din.
Oh, where is the orchestra? From harpist down to
    drummer
They've all disappeared with the passing of the
    summer.

End-of-Summer Poem
Rowena Bastin Bennett

Where the weather is warm, there are always plenty of insects and other many-legged creatures. But in places that turn cold and snowy during winter, these animals seem to vanish. What happens to them? Where do they go?

Most insects, spiders, and other many-legged animals need warmth. When the temperature goes down, these creatures become stiff and cannot move. And many kinds of insects eat green plants. So, they can't live in winter, when there is nothing for them to eat.

Many insects only live from spring until fall. They die as cold weather nears. But many of them mate in autumn, and the females lay eggs. The eggs are fastened to

branches, buried in the ground, or hidden away in safe places. The cold and snow do not harm them. When warm weather comes, in spring or early summer, the eggs hatch. The baby insects come scurrying out to live their one summer of life.

Some insects that hatch from eggs during the summer are still "babies" in the fall. They do not die. Some of them spin a silk cocoon (kuh KOON) around themselves. Others are covered with a kind of shell. They spend the winter inside these coverings, fastened to branches or walls or hidden in the ground. Inside the covering, a great change takes place. In spring, when the insects break out of their covering, they aren't babies anymore. Now they are adults, ready for a new kind of life.

Some kinds of adult many-legged creatures don't die in the fall, either. They creep into sheltered places—beneath a rock, under the loose bark of a tree, beneath a

evergreen bagworm

female hornet

grasshopper eggs

pile of dead leaves. As the days grow colder, the creatures become stiff and stop moving. They are in a kind of frozen sleep, and are just barely alive. But in the spring, as the air warms up, the creatures warm up with it. In time, they are warm enough to begin moving about again.

And some kinds of adult insects do as some kinds of birds do—they fly to a warm place to spend the winter. When summer returns, they, or their "children," come flying back.

praying mantis' egg case

wolf spider

ant nest

Can they think?

When an insect comes out of its egg it is ready for life. It knows what kind of food to eat and how to get it. It knows what certain sounds and smells mean. It doesn't have to learn any of these things. And it doesn't think about them. It is simply able to do them.

An insect's body contains many "messages." As the creature moves about, "messages" tell it what to do next. A certain smell may give it a message to taste. A certain taste will give it a message to eat. And so on. Most of the things an insect does are done because of these messages—not because the insect thought about doing them.

Some insects can learn things. A bee can be taught to go to a certain color for food. And some insects can remember things. A hunter wasp seems to find its way back to its nest by remembering landmarks. So insects have a kind of intelligence. But none of them can think as a human does—or even as well as a dog or cat does.

Insects are very important food for birds and many other creatures.

Are they important?

Insects are *very* important. The world could get along without people—but it *couldn't* get along without insects!

For one thing, insects and other many-legged creatures are important food for many kinds of fish, birds, and other animals. If all the insects were to suddenly vanish, all the creatures that eat them would soon die.

Insects are just as important to many

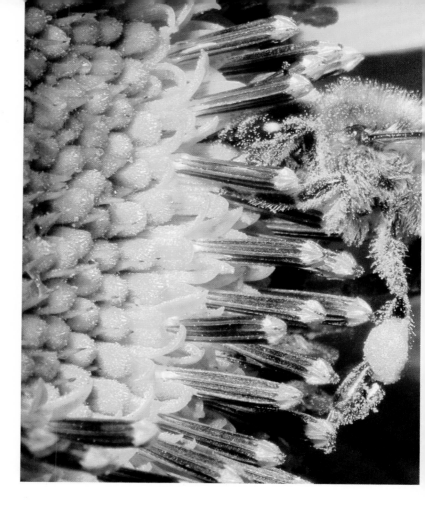

plants. All flowers become some kind of
fruit or vegetable with seeds in it. But to
make this happen, some flowers need pollen
from another flower. And it is insects, such
as butterflies and bees, that bring pollen
from one flower to another.

Thus, without insects, there wouldn't be
many kinds of fruits and vegetables—such
as apples, cherries, oranges, grapes, pears,
carrots, pumpkins, and cucumbers! And, of
course, all these kinds of plants would soon
disappear, because there wouldn't be any
seeds from which new plants could grow.

Many insects that live in the soil help

honeybee on a sunflower

Without bees and other insects many kinds of plants could not grow. A bee gets covered with yellow pollen when it visits a flower. It spreads pollen among all the flowers it visits. This enables the flowers to make seeds.

keep the soil fertile so that plants can grow in it. And many kinds of insects and many-legged animals do important work as nature's garbage collectors. They feed on the remains of dead animals and plants.

Several kinds of insects provide people with useful things. Honey, which is a very good food, is made by bees. Bees also make a wax that people use to make candles, shoe polish, furniture polish, and other things. Silk cloth is made from threads spun by certain kinds of caterpillars. Several kinds of medicine also come from parts of insects' bodies.

We think of all these useful insects as helpful insects. But there are other kinds of insects that we think of as harmful.

Many kinds of insects damage plants and trees by eating parts of them or laying eggs in them. Such insects are a terrible problem to farmers. They destroy food that people need. They also kill useful plants such as cotton. There are also insects that do great damage to wood, to cloth, and to stored foods such as flour, cheese, and meat.

Even worse, some insects are a danger to people because they carry germs that cause diseases. The disease called malaria kills about a million people each year. Malaria is carried by a certain kind of mosquito. A certain kind of fly carries the disease called African sleeping sickness. This disease is a serious problem in Africa. Even ordinary houseflies can carry diseases, as can ticks, lice, and fleas.

damaged redwood tree
Many insects are harmful to plant life. The larvae of bark beetles kill trees by digging tunnels in the trunks and branches.

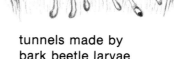

tunnels made by bark beetle larvae

Insects are, indeed, important. Some are important because they cause us serious trouble. Others are important because they are useful to us. But we shouldn't think of insects and other many-legged animals as "good" or "bad." Like all wild creatures, they are simply doing what they must to stay alive. They are part of the great web of life that includes every living plant and animal.

hawk moth and thistle

Insects are an important part of the great web of life that includes all plants and animals.

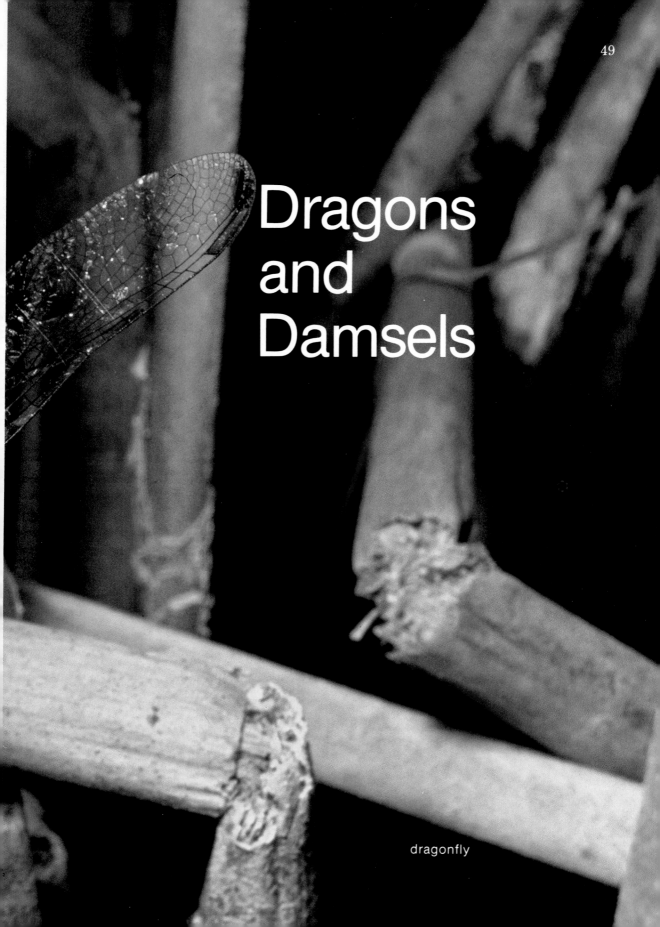

Dragons and Damsels

dragonfly

When the heat of the summer
Made drowsy the land,
A dragon-fly came
And sat on my hand.
With its blue jointed body,
And wings like spun glass,
It lit on my fingers
As though they were grass.

A Dragon-Fly
Eleanor Farjeon

Dragonfly fables

Have you ever seen a "darning needle," or a "horse stinger," or a "mosquito hawk"? You have if you've seen a dragonfly. These are all nicknames for the dragonfly.

Dragonflies have a lot of nicknames. They're often called "darning needles," or "devil's darning needles." People once believed that a dragonfly could use its thin, needlelike body to sew up a person's ears, nose, and mouth!

Dragonflies have also been called "horse stingers" and "mule stingers." Many people think a dragonfly has a dangerous, poisonous sting. But dragonflies do *not* sting. You can hold a dragonfly in your hand or let it cling to your finger. It won't bite you—and it can't sting you.

But dragonflies do attack other insects. They're fierce, swift hunters. They've earned the name "mosquito hawks" because of the way they dart after mosquitoes, seizing them in midair. Dragonflies are also called "bee hawks" and "bee butchers," because they kill and eat many honeybees.

In parts of the United States, some people call dragonflies "snake feeders" and "snake doctors." This is because they think that dragonflies "look after" snakes! Some people even believe that a "snake doctor" can bring a dead snake back to life!

Dragonflies have long, pointed tails. This is why they are often called "darning needles" or "darners".

Dragonflies hunt in the air. They'll attack any kind of flying insect. This dragonfly is eating a butterfly it caught.

The two lives
of a dragonfly

The green stems of plants poke up from the water of the little pond. Inside the stem of one plant, just under the surface of the water, lies a tiny egg. The egg has been in the plant stem for about ten days.

Suddenly, the egg begins to quiver. The little creature inside is breaking out. Using three sharp points on its tail, the creature makes an opening in the egg. Then it pushes its way out and onto the stem of the plant.

The newborn animal has a jointed, greenish-brown body and six legs. Two big, bulgy, yellowish eyes on its large head stare out at the watery world of the pond. It is a baby dragonfly—about to begin the first of its two lives.

The dragonfly baby, or nymph, is all ready for life in the pond, even though it has only just hatched. It breathes through gills in the tip of its tail. It swims by sucking water into its gills, then quickly squirting it out. This makes the nymph shoot forward, just as a balloon does when you let the air squirt out of it.

The nymph knows exactly how to get its food. Clinging to the stem of the plant, it waits. After a time, another creature comes wriggling up through the water. It has a

long, jointed body, but is much smaller than the nymph. It is a mosquito baby, or larva.

The nymph waits, silent and motionless. The mosquito larva comes nearer and nearer. Suddenly, part of the nymph's head seems to shoot out toward the larva! It is like a broad, flat arm with two claws. Actually, this is one of the nymph's mouth parts—the lower lip. Most of the time this lower lip is folded flat on the underside of the nymph's head.

The two claws seize the larva, digging into its soft body. Then the lip folds back, carrying the larva to the nymph's mouth. While the claws hold the larva fast, the nymph begins to chew the helpless larva and stuff the pieces into its mouth!

This is how the nymph spends most of its time. Clinging to a plant stem, it lies in wait for smaller creatures to come along. If the hunting isn't good in one place, it swims to another place.

The nymph is a dreadful danger to the tiny creatures of the pond. But it is also always in danger. There are many larger hunters in the pond, such as giant water

bugs and frogs. Many of the nymph's brothers and sisters are eaten by these creatures. Life in the pond is one of constant danger. It is a struggle to stay alive.

From time to time, the nymph takes off its skin. The skin becomes brittle and splits across the back. With a lot of pushing and wiggling, the nymph pulls itself free. The old skin is left behind, like a pale, hollow statue of the nymph.

Each time the nymph sheds its skin, the nymph is a little bigger. After it has shed its skin several times, little stubby wings appear on its back.

The nymph stays in the pond for about two years. Then, a special day arrives. The nymph is ready to shed its skin for the last time.

The nymph crawls up a plant stem until it is above the water. There it rests in the warm summer sunshine, its six legs gripping the plant stem. Slowly it begins to push its way out of the split in its old skin. Bit by bit, it jerks and wiggles itself free. Then it rests, sitting on top of its old skin, which is as transparent as glass.

During the next half hour, the nymph

slowly grows and changes. Its stubby wings swell until they are long and lacy. The nymph has become a dragonfly—and started the second of its two lives. This second life will last only a few weeks or months.

The dragonfly's body, three inches (7.5 centimeters) long, is soft, pale, and weak. When the dragonfly takes off to make its first flight, it is very wobbly.

But within a week, the dragonfly is strong and has taken on its full color. Its head and the front part of its body are now bright green, which is why this dragonfly is often called a "green darner." It is an active, powerful dragon of the air, that skims swiftly over pond and shore. At times, it hovers in one place, like a helicopter. It busily searches for prey. It seldom stops to rest.

The dragonfly's big, keen eyes catch sight of a mosquito humming through the air. At once, the dragonfly spreads its legs to form a basket. It rushes upon the mosquito at a speed of nearly thirty miles (50 kilometers) an hour. Slamming into the mosquito, it scoops the surprised creature into its basket of legs and begins to devour it! The dragonfly doesn't sit down to eat, it keeps right on flying.

The dragonfly now has a different kind of mouth than it had when it was a nymph. Its

lower lip is shaped like a bowl, with hooks around the edge. The dragonfly uses this lip like a plate. The hooks hold the mosquito while the dragonfly chews it to pieces.

The dragonfly is now a terror of the air, just as it was a terror of the pond when it was a nymph. But, just as it was always in danger as a nymph, it is also in danger as a dragonfly. At any moment, it may be snatched out of the air by a hungry bird. And, if it stops to rest on a leaf or plant stem, a bullfrog may gobble it up.

For several weeks, the dragonfly, which is a female, spends the warm summer days flying about. At times she alights on a plant stem and clings there, to rest. But she seldom walks.

Finally, the time comes when the dragonfly is ready to mate. There are eggs in her body. As she flies, a male dragonfly comes to join her. Still flying, the two of them cling together and mate in the air.

Then, still clinging together, the two tiny, gleaming dragons sail down toward the surface of the pond. They hover beside the stem of a plant growing up out of the water. The female dips her long tail into the water, and pushes it into the stem of the plant. She lays one of her eggs inside the plant. There, it will be safe and protected. Soon, a little nymph will hatch—ready to begin the first of its two lives.

Damselflies

Damselflies are cousins of dragonflies and are often called narrow-winged dragonflies. The word *damsel* means "a slim, young girl," and damselflies are smaller and slimmer than dragonflies.

Like dragonflies, damselflies are fierce hunters and skim close to the water of streams and ponds in search of prey. Their way of life is much like that of dragonflies.

a damselfly

Damselflies and dragonflies look much alike. But when a damselfly rests, it holds its wings together. A resting dragonfly holds its wings straight out.

The Beetle Bunch

scarab beetles

Lady-bird! Lady-bird! fly away home;
  The field mouse is gone to her nest,
The daisies have shut up their sleepy red eyes,
  And the birds and the bees are at rest.

Lady-bird! Lady-bird! fly away home;
  The glow-worm is lighting her lamp,
The dew's falling fast, and your fine speckled wings
  Will flag with the close-clinging damp.

Lady-bird! Lady-bird! fly away home;
  The fairy-bells tinkle afar;
Make haste, or they'll catch you and harness you fast
  With a cobweb to Oberon's car.

To the Lady-Bird
Author Unknown

The plant protectors

The plant leaf is covered with tiny green insects. These insects, called aphids (AY fihdz), suck juices out of plants. In time, they will kill this plant!

But, suddenly, a flying creature alights on the leaf and folds its wings with a click. It is a round-bodied, red-and-black ladybug.

The ladybug is quite a bit bigger than the aphids. Marching to the nearest aphid, the ladybug seizes it and gobbles it down! One after another, the ladybug eats the aphids until all are gone!

Ladybugs are also called ladybirds and lady beetles.Why? Hundreds of years ago, people saw how useful these beetles were. So, they named them for Mary, the mother of Jesus, who is often called Our Lady.

Ladybugs are very useful. They eat aphids and other insects that destroy many kinds of plants we use for food. Many years ago, aphids threatened to destroy the fruit crop in California. But the fruit was saved by turning thousands of ladybugs loose.

There are about four thousand different kinds of ladybugs in the world. Many are red or yellow with black spots. Some are black with red or yellow spots. Their bright colors are probably a "warning" to birds that ladybugs taste bad. And, birds usually leave them alone.

The bright-colored back of a ladybug is really two, hard wing covers. If you watch a ladybug getting ready to fly, you'll see its colored back split in two as it lifts its wing covers out of the way of its wings. Most kinds of beetles have wing covers. Wing covers are one of the things that make them beetles.

ladybug and aphids

Tiger beetles

Many of the beetles you see scuttling about on a warm, sunny day are probably tiger beetles. They're called tigers because they hunt like tigers. They creep up on a smaller insect, then rush at it, seize it, and munch it up!

A mother tiger beetle digs tunnels and lays one egg in each. The larvae that hatch out look like long-legged caterpillars. Like their parents, they're meat-eaters. But they have a different way of hunting. After a larva hatches, it lies in wait just inside the entrance to its tunnel. When an insect passes close by, the larva rears out and grabs it. Then the larva pulls its captive into the tunnel and has dinner!

There are many kinds of tiger beetles. Most of them are brightly colored and shiny. You can find some kinds on sandy beaches, some in woods, and some in gardens—where they help to keep out harmful pests.

Flying flashlights

It is a summer evening, just at twilight. The grassy meadow and nearby forest are filling with shadows. Suddenly, scores of tiny, flashing lights drift through the gathering darkness. The fireflies have come out.

Fireflies, also known as lightning bugs, are neither flies nor bugs. They are really beetles. You can often see them during the day, crawling or resting on leaves. At twilight, the males begin to fly and flash their lights. The females flash their lights in answer. The flashing lights are a signal that helps male and female fireflies find each other, so they can mate.

A firefly's light comes from the underside of the firefly's body, near the back end. A firefly has special chemicals in its body. When these chemicals mix with oxygen, a gas that is in the air, the firefly is able to make a light. This light is a cold light— there is almost no heat. It is not like the lights we know how to make, which give off heat as well as light.

Baby fireflies, or larvae, hatch from eggs. These babies, which look somewhat like caterpillars, are fierce hunters! At night, they creep beneath loose earth and dead leaves in search of snails, worms, and the larvae of other insects. A firefly larva shoots poison into its prey with its mouthparts. The

poison turns the creature's insides to liquid, which the larva then sucks out.

A few kinds of adult fireflies are also hunters. But many kinds don't eat at all. They live only to mate. Then they die.

Some kinds of female fireflies don't have wings. They look much like caterpillars. In some places these wingless fireflies are called glowworms.

A beetle with a "cannon"!

Squatting in a woods, a frog watches a dark, shiny beetle with a red head. When the beetle is close enough, the frog jumps at it. The frog's sticky tongue shoots out. The beetle sticks to it and is pulled into the frog's mouth.

But, as the frog's tongue touches the beetle, there is a muffled *pop*. It sounds like a tiny cannon being fired. Instantly, the frog spits out the beetle and begins to choke and gag. The beetle scurries away.

The unlucky frog has tried to eat a bombardier (bahm buh DEER) beetle. But this kind of beetle is well able to defend itself. The word *bombardier* originally meant "one who fires a cannon."

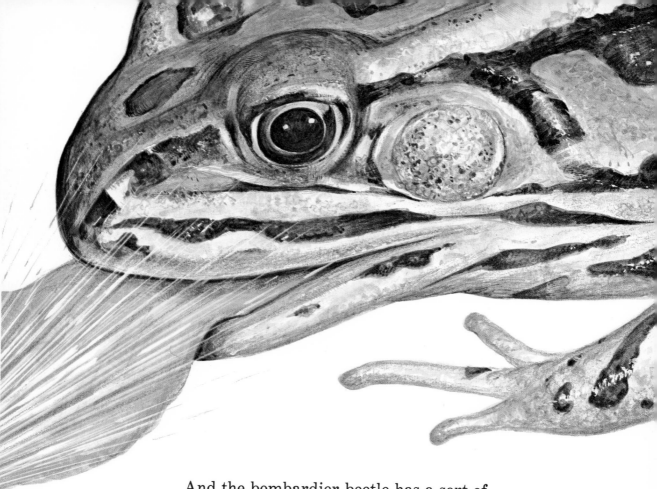

And the bombardier beetle has a sort of cannon in its back end! It can shoot out a burning, stinging cloud of liquid. Any bird, reptile, or other creature that gets a blast from the beetle's cannon in its mouth will drop the beetle at once!

The bombardier beetle is quite common in many parts of the United States and Canada. A bombardier beetle that is black with four yellow spots is common in Australia.

Bombardier beetles are about half an inch (12.5 millimeters) long. These insects are useful. They eat many kinds of harmful insects. One kind is the gypsy moth caterpillar, which destroys trees.

Snout beetles

If you ever happen to see a beetle that looks as if it has a very long nose, it is probably a snout beetle. Snout beetles are also known as weevils.

The snout isn't a nose. It is actually a long mouth, with jaws at the end. Having such a long mouth enables a snout beetle to chew deep into things. Mother snout beetles chew deep tunnels into nuts, fruits, seeds, and the stems and roots of plants. Then they lay eggs in the tunnels. When the larvae hatch, they have all the food they need.

The snout beetle family is the biggest of all the animal families in the world! There

snout beetle
The mouth of a snout beetle, or weevil, is a long tube with jaws at the tip. The beetle uses its mouth like a drill, to bore into seeds and buds.

are at least forty thousand different kinds of these creatures. That's more than all the different kinds of birds, reptiles, amphibians (frogs and toads), and mammals (furry animals) put together!

Unfortunately, many kinds of snout beetles are pests. They are almost all plant-eaters, and many of them eat plants that we use for food or other things. Snout beetles spoil many kinds of fruits, nuts, seeds, grain, and vegetables. Some kill trees. One kind, called a boll weevil, does terrible damage to cotton plants.

However, some snout beetles are a help to us. We use them to kill plants that are growing where they aren't wanted.

Beetle gravediggers!

A dead mouse lies in a meadow. With a
whir of wings, a brightly colored beetle
lands beside it. Squeezing under the body,
the beetle begins to dig.

After a time, another beetle appears,
winging through the air. It circles about
until it locates the dead mouse. Then it lands
and begins to help the first beetle dig.

Soon, a number of the same kind of
beetles are busily at work, digging the dirt
out from beneath the mouse. Slowly, the
mouse's body sinks down into the hole. As it
sinks deeper, loose dirt begins to cover it up.
In a few hours, the mouse is buried. And two
of the beetles, a male and a female have
buried themselves with it—after driving off
the others.

These beetles are known as burying
beetles. They are able to smell the odor of a
dead mouse, snake, or other creature from a
long way off. They bury small, dead
creatures so that they will have a hidden
store of food, all to themselves. The beetles
feed on the dead creature, and mother
beetles lay their eggs on it. When the beetle
larvae hatch, they eat the dead animal, too.

Burying beetles work hard for their food.
If they find a dead creature on hard, rocky
ground, where they can't dig, they will drag
it to a softer spot!

Water tigers!

A tiny tadpole—a baby frog—swims slowly
in the water of a quiet stream. Suddenly, a
long, jointed shape rushes toward it. Sharp,
curved jaws bite into the tadpole's body and
hold it fast. The tadpole has been caught by
a water tiger!

Water tigers are the larvae of beetles
known as diving beetles. These larvae will

attack almost anything, even creatures larger than themselves. They eat other insects, snails, tadpoles, fish, and even other water tigers!

Water tigers shoot a poisonous liquid into their victims. The liquid turns a creature's insides to a liquid. The water tiger then sucks the juice out through its hollow jaws.

Although water tigers live in water, they have to breathe air. From time to time they

diving beetle

swim up to the top of the water. They take in air through the back end of the body.

When a water tiger is ready to become a diving beetle, it creeps up onto land. It digs a little burrow in the earth. Hidden inside the burrow, it begins to change. If it leaves the water in the middle of summer, it will change into a beetle in about three weeks. But if it comes out in the autumn, it will hibernate in the burrow all winter. Then it will become a beetle in the spring.

The diving beetle has a flat, tear-shaped body. It spends most of its time in the water. Before it dives, it fills a space under its wing covers with air. When it needs more air, it rises to the top of the water.

The diving beetle is a fine swimmer. It uses its two, strong, flat, and hairy back legs like oars. It swims swiftly after prey, for it is as fierce a hunter as it was when it was a larva. But now it has a different way of eating. Instead of sucking liquid out of the creatures it catches, it tears them to pieces and chews up the bits.

Diving beetles often hang upside down in the water, with their back ends poking into the air. At times, on a summer night, diving beetles may leave their watery home and fly in search of a new one. They are good fliers. But if a diving beetle should chance to land on the ground, it is clumsy and awkward when it tries to walk.

water scavenger beetle

Diving beetles aren't the only beetles that can swim.
The beetles called water scavenger beetles are good
swimmers, too. When this beetle dives, it carries air
bubbles under its body, as the picture shows. These
beetles eat dead plants and animals.

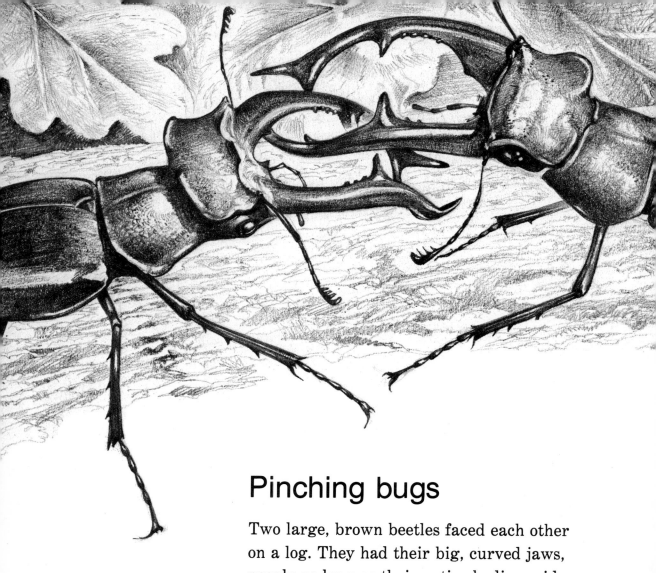

Pinching bugs

Two large, brown beetles faced each other on a log. They had their big, curved jaws, nearly as long as their entire bodies, wide open.

Suddenly, one beetle charged! The beetles bumped together, struggling and pushing and clicking their jaws. Finally, one beetle tumbled backward and slipped off the log. The fight was over. Nearby, a female beetle was waiting. The fight had been over her! She would now be the winner's mate.

These big-jawed beetles are called stag beetles. This is because their jaws look like the antlers of a stag, or male deer. Only the

males have these big jaws. Scientists aren't
sure why, because the jaws aren't good for
much. They are so big and awkward that they
often seem to get in the way. But they don't
prevent the beetles from flying.

Some people call these beetles pinching
bugs because the jaws look as if they ought
to be able to give a good pinch. Actually, the
big jaws of the males are quite weak. But
the females, which have much smaller jaws,
can really give you a pinch—one that will
make your finger bleed!

Stag beetles look fierce, but they aren't.
They feed mostly on sap that oozes out of
trees. Stag beetle larvae look like fat, white
worms. The larvae eat the rotting wood of
old logs and stumps, where the mother
beetles lay their eggs.

Beetle giants

Goliath beetles

Goliath beetles live in Africa. They are about four inches (10 cm) long, and are the heaviest of all insects. They eat mostly nectar and pollen. The one on the left is a female, the other is a male.

Hercules beetle

This male Hercules beetle from South America is about six inches (15 cm) long. The males use their long horns in "duels" with each other. The females have very small horns or none at all.

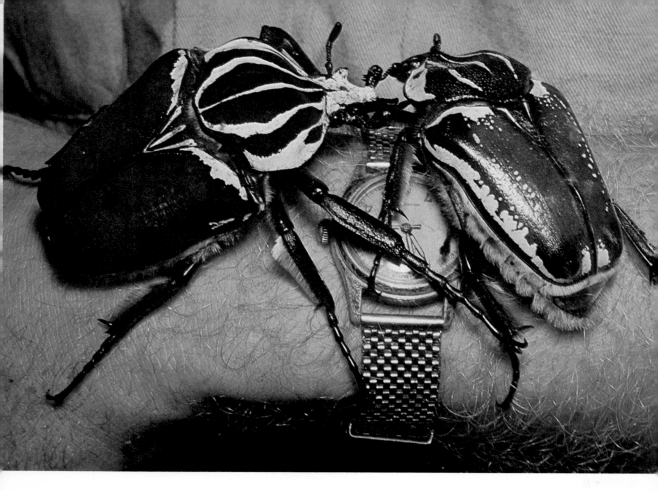

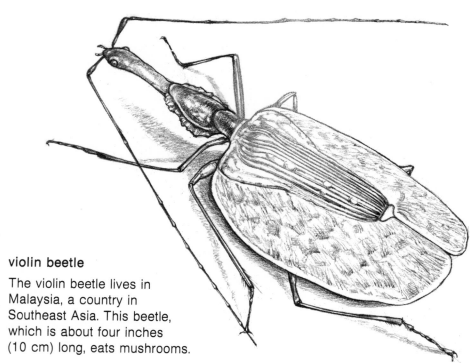

violin beetle

The violin beetle lives in
Malaysia, a country in
Southeast Asia. This beetle,
which is about four inches
(10 cm) long, eats mushrooms.

The Grasshopper Group

grasshopper

Grasshopper Green is a comical chap;
  He lives on the best of fare.
Bright little trousers, jacket, and cap,
  These are his summer wear.
Out in the meadow he loves to go,
  Playing away in the sun;
It's hopperty, skipperty, high and low,
  Summer's the time for fun.

Grasshopper Green has a quaint little house;
  It's under the hedge so gay.
Grandmother Spider, as still as a mouse,
  Watches him over the way.
Gladly he's calling the children, I know,
  Out in the beautiful sun;
It's hopperty, skipperty, high and low,
  Summer's the time for fun.

Grasshopper Green
Author Unknown

The life of a grasshopper

It is September. The air is warm and sunny. The trees are green and shaggy with leaves. In a golden, grassy meadow, a mother grasshopper is ready to lay her eggs.

At the end of her long tail are several hard, sharp points. She pushes these into the ground, drilling into the soft dirt. Stretching out her tail, she makes a long, deep hole. Then, from the end of her tail, she drops a number of tiny eggs into the bottom of the hole.

A foamy, sticky stuff comes out of the grasshopper's tail along with the eggs. This sticky stuff quickly dries, covering all the eggs. It is like a sponge, full of holes through which air can reach the eggs.

Now, with a great leap, the grasshopper soars away. She will dig several more holes and lay more clumps of eggs. Each clump may hold from twenty to seventy eggs. At this time of year, a great many mother grasshoppers are laying eggs, so there are thousands of eggs buried in the meadow.

Many of these eggs will never hatch. The meadow is filled with the larvae of blister beetles and several kinds of flies—creatures that eat grasshopper eggs. But they don't find all the eggs.

Autumn comes to the meadow. The leaves change color and drop from the trees. The

green, juicy plants of summer turn to dry, withered husks. The adult grasshoppers are all dead. After a time, snow falls. The ground freezes.

The cold of winter actually makes the tiny creatures inside the eggs begin to grow. This is nature's way of helping them. If the eggs simply needed warmth to hatch, they might hatch too soon. Then the baby grasshoppers would be caught without food at the beginning of winter. (Of course, grasshoppers that live in places where it's always warm and where there are always plants growing don't have this problem. They can hatch at anytime.)

Winter comes to an end. The spring sun warms the meadow. New green plants begin to push up out of the earth. Inside their eggs, the baby grasshoppers begin to stir. They are ready to come out into a world that will be warm and full of food.

One of the eggs splits at the top. The baby grasshopper pushes its way out. It is wrapped in a sort of loose skin that holds the grasshopper's legs against its body. The grasshopper crawls upward, like a worm, through the tunnels and holes of the material that forms the clump of eggs. It pushes its way through the dirt. Finally, it breaks out into the air and light.

The crawling and pushing causes the wrapper of loose skin to split. The skin shrinks and slides off. Now the baby can stand up on its six legs. Unlike many baby insects, it looks like its parents, except that it has no wings.

As if to celebrate its new life, the little creature makes a mighty four-inch (10-centimeter) jump. This is really a gigantic leap! It would be about 120 feet (36 meters) for a tall person!

The young grasshopper's main interest is food. Different kinds of grasshoppers eat different things. Many kinds eat grass. But some eat garden plants and farm crops.

The young grasshopper eats and grows. It has to crawl out of its outer skin about six

Male grasshoppers make "music" by rubbing their front wings and back legs together.

times during the first six weeks of its life. Each time, its body is longer and its wings have grown a bit. The last time, its wings swell up and become full size. The grasshopper is now full grown. It may be one to two inches (2.5 to 5 cm) long, depending on the kind of grasshopper it is.

Almost every minute of its life, the grasshopper is in danger. A bird may swoop down on it, or it may be seized by another insect. Frogs, toads, and snakes will gladly gobble it up. So will raccoons and skunks. And some kinds of wasps hunt female grasshoppers. They carry them off to be food for baby wasps.

The grasshopper's best defense is to make one of its long jumps. It does this with its wings spread, to carry it in a great, curving glide. Its greenish or brownish color also helps it to hide in grass or among leaves.

Throughout the long, warm days of summer, the grasshopper walks, hops, and glides about in the meadow. Because it eats grass, it has plenty of food.

This grasshopper is a male, so it can make "music." As it flies, it makes a crackling sound. It does this by rubbing its front wings and back legs together. On each back leg there is a "scraper." This is like a tiny comb with many teeth. And each wing has a thick ridge. The grasshopper makes its "song" by rubbing the scrapers against

the ridges. Sometimes it does this while standing in the grass.

Near the end of summer, a female grasshopper is attracted to the male's song. She comes to where he is. They stand facing each other, their short antennae, or feelers, touching. It is almost as if they are getting acquainted. They meet this way for several days. Finally, one day, they mate. Soon, the female will lay her eggs.

The male grasshopper keeps making his music for a time. But as the days pass, he makes it less and less often. And it becomes softer and softer. After about a week, it stops.

The grasshopper no longer eats. Soon, he stops moving. His short summer of life in the sunny meadow has come to an end.

locusts eating corn plants

The kind of grasshoppers
called locusts sometimes
gather in huge swarms.
Such swarms destroy huge
amounts of crops.

Grasshopper trouble!

Grasshoppers often cause trouble—terrible trouble! Sometimes enormous numbers of grasshoppers hatch at about the same time. They begin to move across the land, eating as they go. Soon, they are able to fly. When they all take off in a gigantic swarm, billions of grasshoppers darken the sky!

Where one of these swarms comes down, there is dreadful destruction! The billions of grasshoppers eat every green plant and leaf in their path. They can destroy hundreds of square miles (square kilometers) of farm crops. If they come to a town, they often fill the streets in such numbers that people can't walk or drive. Parts of rivers may even become filled up with the bodies of dead grasshoppers.

The grasshoppers that cause all of this trouble and damage are called locusts. They are the kind of grasshopper known as short-horned grasshoppers because they have short feelers, or "horns." No one knows why so many of them sometimes appear so suddenly.

katydid

Katydid-katydidn't

On hot summer nights, the air is often filled
with a noise that, to some people, sounds
like *katydid-katydidn't-katydid-katydidn't*.
This sound is made by the kind of
grasshopper called a katydid. Katydids are
also known as long-horned grasshoppers,
because they have long feelers, or "horns."

Although you can hear katydids, you
seldom see them. That's because they're
usually high in the trees. Their wings look
like leaves, and their bodies are green, so
they blend right in.

Long-horned grasshoppers don't make
their "music" the way short-horned
grasshoppers do. Instead of rubbing their
back legs against their front wings, they
rub a sharp edge on one front wing against
a row of bumps on the other front wing.
Usually only the males make a noise. They
do this to attract females.

That praying mantis over there
is really not engaged in prayer.
That praying mantis that you see
is really preying (with an "e").
It preys upon the garter snake.
It preys upon the bumblebee.
It preys upon the cabbage worm,
The wasp, the fly, the moth, the flea.
(And sometimes, if its need is great,
it even preys upon its mate.)

With prey and preying both so endless,
It tends to end up rather friendless
And seldom is commended much
Except by gardeners and such.

Praying Mantis
Mary Ann Hoberman

A "praying" hunter

A large green insect stands in a clump of grass. It blends into the grass so well it can hardly be seen. Its little head twists and turns in all directions, as if the creature were searching for something.

The insect stands on its middle and back legs. It holds its front legs up, folded together in front of its "chest." The creature looks as if it were praying!

Suddenly, the insect's head stops moving. It has seen something. A grasshopper is coming toward it.

The grasshopper is slightly bigger than the hidden insect—but that doesn't matter. The insect darts from its hiding place. In a flash, its folded legs open up, stretch out, and snap shut on the grasshopper. The legs are like jaws with sharp teeth. They hold the startled grasshopper so that it can't move. The insect bites the back of the grasshopper's head, killing it. Then, the creature starts to eat the grasshopper. Soon, only a few scattered bits are left!

The insect is called a mantid. It is also known as a praying mantis, because it often looks as if it were praying. But when it seems to be praying, it is really hunting— and it hunts most of the time! Mantids are such fierce and greedy flesh-eaters that they are sometimes called "insect tyrannosaurs"!

mantid

If a mantid thinks it is in danger, it spreads its front legs and wings just as this mantid is doing.

But they are very helpful to farmers and gardeners because they eat a great many insect pests.

A mantid will eat until it's stuffed—and then will catch another creature and start eating again! It won't hesitate to attack something bigger than it is. The largest mantids will eat birds, frogs, and small lizards. Mantids even eat other mantids. And a female mantid will usually eat the male with whom she has just mated!

There are many different kinds of mantids. Most are disguised in ways that

help them to hide. Many are green, and blend into grass or leaves. Some look like bits of tree bark. Some are long and thin, like twigs. Some are brightly colored, and hide among flowers. These mantids look so much like flowers that an insect doesn't notice them—until it is too late!

Mantids are large insects. Some kinds are as much as five inches (12.5 centimeters) long. Mantids are also one of the few kinds of insects that can be made into pets! They can be taught to take bits of raw meat or fruit from a person's fingers.

A walking stick, or stick insect, looks like a twig.

Walking sticks

Many people have seen what they thought was part of a bush suddenly start to walk! What they thought was a twig sticking up from a branch was really an insect that looks like a twig.

Most people call these skinny, twiglike insects walking sticks. Walking sticks belong to the same group of insects as grasshoppers. However, many kinds can't jump or fly as grasshoppers do—they have no wings. They live mostly in trees or bushes.

Most kinds of walking sticks in North America are only about two inches (5 centimeters) long. But in Australia there is a stick insect about ten inches (25 cm) long. And in Malaysia there is a stick insect more than a foot (30 cm) long!

Cheerful chirpers

Crickets are the main music makers of the insect world. The steady *chirp-chirp-chirp* you often hear on a warm night is cricket music. Crickets make their music by rubbing the sharp edge on one wing against a row of bumps on the other wing.

There are many kinds of crickets. One kind, house crickets, likes to live in people's houses. Black, big-headed field crickets live in meadows and lawns, but they often come into houses. Tree crickets stay in trees and bushes. There are crickets that live in caves, and crickets that live in ant nests—and are fed by the ants!

Most kinds of crickets are night animals. During the day they find a place to hide. At night they come out to eat. Field crickets eat grass, fruits, grain, and dead insects. House crickets will eat almost any kind of food. Tree crickets eat aphids, the tiny insects that live on leaves.

The tunnel digger

Down in the damp, dark earth, a mole cricket is digging its way along. This cricket got its name because it's a lot like a mole. A mole is a brown, furry animal that lives underground and digs tunnels. And a mole cricket is a brown, furry insect that lives underground and digs tunnels.

The mole cricket's front feet are like broad shovels with four sharp points. The cricket uses these feet to scoop earth from in front of itself as it moves through the ground. It makes long tunnels that are usually about six or eight inches (15 to 20 centimeters) below the ground.

As it shovels along in the darkness, the cricket may bump into another creature. If it does, it will try to eat the creature. But if the cricket bumps into a mole, the cricket will get eaten.

Young mole crickets eat plant roots. Because this kills the plants, farmers and gardeners don't like mole crickets.

Male mole crickets looking for a mate come up out of the ground to sit and chirp. And, although these crickets spend most of their time underground, they are good fliers. They sometimes come out at night and go on long flights. They are attracted to lights, so you may sometimes see a mole cricket crawling on a street light.

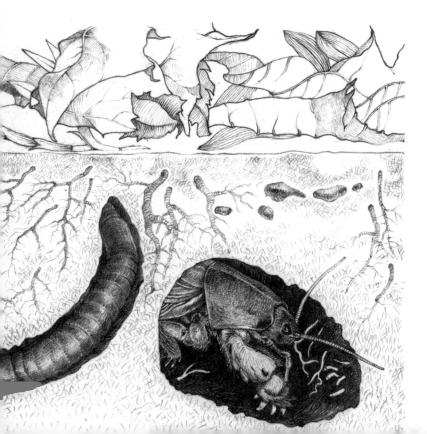

A mole cricket spends most of its time underground. But it comes above ground to search for a mate.

A "prehistoric" pest

Would you like to see a *live* "prehistoric" animal—one that lived long before the dinosaurs? Well, look at a cockroach!

There were cockroaches swarming in hot, damp forests more than three hundred million years ago! And cockroaches have hardly changed a bit since. They are what scientists call a "successful living creature." This means they have not had to change their way of life for millions of years.

Many things help cockroaches survive. For one thing, a cockroach is a very fast runner. And its body is flat and slippery, so it can quickly slide into cracks that most other creatures can't get into.

Cockroaches will eat almost anything— human food, garbage, dead plants and animals, cloth, leather, even wood. This has helped them survive. An animal that eats only one thing—such as a certain kind of plant—doesn't have as much chance to survive as does an animal that eats many things.

Mother cockroaches don't lay "bare" eggs, as most insects do. Their eggs are protected inside a hard container that looks like a tiny purse. Some kinds of roaches even disguise these containers so that they look like lumps of dirt. Others keep the containers with them until the eggs hatch. All this helps

cockroach

keep roach eggs from being eaten by other creatures. Some kinds of roaches give birth to live babies, just as humans do. This, too, has helped cockroaches survive.

Most kinds of cockroaches live out of doors and never come near people. During the day they hide under rocks or in the loose bark of trees. At night they come out to eat dead plants or animals.

But, a few kinds of cockroaches do live in houses and buildings. They, too, hide during the day. At night they come out to eat. They chew cloth, books, and other things, often ruining them. They get into people's food and spoil it. And they may spread germs.

Cockroaches are troublesome, dangerous house pests. Everyone hates them, but no one has found a good way to get rid of them. However, house cockroaches do have one deadly enemy—the many-legged centipede. A centipede in the house can be a very useful friend in keeping roaches out.

The Beautiful Ones

butterfly

Fuzzy wuzzy, creepy crawly
   Caterpillar funny,
You will be a butterfly
   When the days are sunny.
Winging, flinging, dancing, springing
   Butterfly so yellow,
You were once a caterpillar,
   Wriggly, wiggly fellow.

Fuzzy Wuzzy, Creepy Crawly
Lilian Schulz Vanada

Butterflies and moths

A fuzzy, creepy, crawly caterpillar may
turn into a butterfly, just as the poem says.
But it might turn into a moth. Moths and
butterflies are very much alike. They both
start life as caterpillars. Often, only an
expert can tell if a caterpillar will turn into
a butterfly or a moth.

When a caterpillar starts to change into a
butterfly or moth, it becomes what is called
a pupa (PYOO puh). Sometimes, you can tell
if a caterpillar will be a moth or butterfly
by the way it becomes a pupa.

Most butterfly caterpillars fasten their
tail to a branch or stem and hang head
down. A kind of shell forms around them.
This shell is called a chrysalis (KRIHS uh
lihs). Inside the chrysalis, the crawly
caterpillar becomes a butterfly.

Many kinds of moth caterpillars spin a
covering of silk around themselves. This
covering is called a cocoon (kuh KOON).
You'll often see cocoons on tree trunks and
branches, on the sides of houses, and other
places. Inside each cocoon, a crawly
caterpillar is becoming a moth.

When caterpillars become butterflies or
moths, it's still hard to tell which is which.
Butterflies and moths both have the same
kind of wings and body shape. Many moths

The antennae of a butterfly (left) usually have little knobs on the ends. The antennae of a moth (right) often look like little feathers.

are small, brown, and not very colorful—but so are many butterflies. Many butterflies are large, brightly colored beauties—but so are many moths. In fact, one of the most beautiful of all living things is a certain kind of moth. There is a picture of this beautiful moth on page 120.

One way you can sometimes tell a butterfly from a moth is by the antennae. A butterfly's antennae always have a knob, or swelling, on the end. Most moths have antennae that either come to a point or that look like tiny feathers. No butterfly has such feathery feelers.

So, the next time you see a pair of colorful wings fluttering over a flower, don't be too sure it's a butterfly. It may be a moth. Look at its antennae and see if you can tell if it's a butterfly or a moth.

The life of a monarch caterpillar

There is a flutter of color in the warm spring air. An orange and black monarch butterfly is flying northward. Below her, a young milkweed plant grows by the side of the road. Its broad leaves shiver slightly in the breeze.

The butterfly flutters down and lands on one of the milkweed leaves. She crawls around to the underside of the leaf. There she lays several eggs. They are sticky and hold fast to the leaf.

The eggs are so tiny you would never notice them. They look like little Christmas tree ornaments. They are a gleaming yellowish-white and are covered with long rows of little bumps, like the kernels on an ear of corn.

The butterfly soars on her way. She has done her job. The eggs are in a safe place. On the underside of the leaf they are protected and hidden from creatures that might eat them. And when the babies hatch, they will have plenty of food. Milkweed leaves are what they eat.

Four days later, the first egg hatches. A pale yellowish-white caterpillar with a black head comes out of it. The caterpillar is about as thick as a bit of thread and as

long as a pinhead is wide. It has sixteen stubby legs and twelve eyes—six on each side of its head! But even with all these eyes, it can't do much more than tell light from darkness.

The first thing the caterpillar does is eat the shell of the egg it has come out of. Now that the shell is empty, it looks like clear glass. The caterpillar munches on the shell with its short, strong jaws.

Next, the caterpillar begins to eat the leaf. For it, the leaf is like a broad, rough meadow! The caterpillar crawls along, munching as it goes. It crawls with its ten soft, lumpy back legs. It doesn't use its six front legs, which are stiff and pointed.

As the caterpillar crawls, liquid from its mouth oozes onto the leaf. As this liquid hits the air, it becomes a thread of silk. The silk thread sticks to the leaf. As the caterpillar

moves along, it leaves a trail of silk. This silken trail is important to the caterpillar. The claws on the caterpillar's feet hold on to the thread as the caterpillar crawls. It can't slip and fall as long as it has this rough, sticky path on which to walk.

The caterpillar eats and eats and grows and grows. Two days later, it has grown so much that its skin splits. The caterpillar crawls out of the skin. It waits for a while, then crawls off to start eating again.

The caterpillar keeps eating and growing and leaving its skin from time to time. Before long, it has colorful yellow, black, and white stripes. It is now big enough and bright enough so that it is easily seen. But,

strangely, its bright colors protect it from some creatures. Most birds quickly learn that bright colors on an insect mean a bad taste. So they leave bright-colored crawlers, such as the caterpillar, alone.

But the caterpillar has one bad scare! A beetle crawls onto the leaf where the caterpillar is eating. For some beetles, a caterpillar is food! The caterpillar senses danger. At once, it lets itself fall off the leaf!

But as it falls, the liquid oozing from its mouth keeps forming silk thread. And this thread is still connected to the trail of thread on the leaf. So the caterpillar doesn't fall to the ground. It hangs by a length of thread, a short distance below the leaf. But to the beetle, the caterpillar has vanished. The beetle takes wing and flies away.

After a time, the caterpillar climbs back up the thread. To get rid of the long piece of thread, which it no longer needs, the caterpillar eats it as it climbs! When the caterpillar reaches the leaf, it crawls on its way as if nothing had happened.

The caterpillar also has another way of protecting itself if it must. Behind its head and above its back pair of legs are two long, pointed "whips." If something touches the caterpillar, it lashes these "whips" furiously. They can't do any real damage, but they will frighten some creatures away.

After a little more than two weeks, the

caterpillar is two inches (5 centimeters) long. It has grown as much as it is going to.

Now it stops eating. It crawls onto the underside of a leaf of the milkweed plant where it has been living. It puts a little knob of sticky silk on the leaf's thick stem. The caterpillar attaches its tail to this knob. Then it lets itself swing out until it hangs head down from the stem.

A day goes by. The caterpillar's skin begins to split. It peels away, shriveling up toward the caterpillar's tail. But what was under the skin no longer looks like a caterpillar. It is a shapeless lump that hardens into a blue-green shell, called a chrysalis, that is flecked with patches of gold and silver!

When a monarch caterpillar is ready to become a butterfly, it hangs head down from a twig. Its skin peels off. The caterpillar is now pale, and very different in shape. A hard shell, called a chrysalis, forms around it. Inside the chrysalis, the caterpillar slowly changes into a butterfly.

A monarch butterfly breaks out of its chrysalis after about twelve days. It clings to the chrysalis while its wings swell up and dry off. Then it flies away.

For a dozen days, the chrysalis hangs from the leaf. It does not change. But, inside it, tremendous changes are taking place! The caterpillar's whole body is changing into something very different!

On the twelfth day, a crack appears in the chrysalis. The crack widens. Something pushes out through the crack. A struggling shape crawls out onto the chrysalis, which now looks like a piece of clear plastic.

The creature clinging to the empty chrysalis has six long legs. It also has long feelers. Its body is black, but there are orange objects on its back, like small, twisted rags.

Slowly, the "rags" swell out. They become a pair of beautiful orange and black wings, with a border of white dots. The crawling caterpillar has become a winged creature of the air—a monarch butterfly.

After a time, the new butterfly soars into the air. Now it begins a new kind of life.

The life of a monarch butterfly

As the new monarch butterfly wings on its way, a sweet odor attracts its attention. Following the odor, it lands on a milkweed. The plant's pinkish flowers are in bloom. Their sweet smell invites the butterfly to come and eat.

The butterfly does not eat the way it did when it was a caterpillar. The caterpillar munched bits of milkweed leaf with its powerful jaws. But the butterfly sips sweet syrup from the milkweed flowers.

The butterfly has a tongue like a long tube. This tongue is coiled up under its mouth. When the butterfly pokes its head into a flower, the tube uncoils. It becomes a long sipper that reaches down to the tiny pool of syrup at the bottom of the flower.

The butterfly spends its days flying and eating. It never walks on the ground. Its long, thin legs are too weak for walking.

Monarch butterflies live in North America, Australia, and a number of other places. Their way of life is the same everywhere. But the North American monarchs do one thing differently. When autumn comes, all the monarchs fly south to one place in Mexico. They migrate, just as many birds do.

migrating monarch butterflies resting on a tree

So, when the sunny days grow shorter and the leaves start to change color, the butterfly heads south. It is joined by many others of its kind. All across the land, large flocks of monarch butterflies sail toward the south.

At times, the butterflies stop to rest. Many thousands gather together in the same tree to spend the night. The tree looks as if it is growing butterflies from its branches, rather than leaves!

Finally, the butterfly reaches a place far south, in Mexico. There, too, it spends its days flying and eating. But it also mates.

After several months, the butterfly begins to move north. It does not travel in a flock, now. It flies alone.

By the time the butterfly reaches the southern part of the United States, it is spring. The butterfly looks different now. Its bright orange wings have become a pale tan. The butterfly does not get back to the place where it spent the last summer. On the way, it dies.

But, on their way north, many female butterflies have laid eggs. The eggs hatch into caterpillars, and the caterpillars become butterflies. These butterflies continue the journey north. And it is these butterflies that will fly south in autumn.

North American monarch butterflies migrate south from Canada to Mexico in the fall. In the spring, they migrate back north for the summer.

Butterfly beauties

peacock butterfly, Spain

Indian leaf butterfly

When this Asian butterfly sits
on a twig and folds its wings
to show the undersides, it
looks like a dead leaf. But the
tops of its wings are colorful.

88 butterfly

The 88 butterfly lives in Peru. It got its name from the
design that looks like the number 88, on the underside
of each of its wings.

A moth beauty

African moth

Many people think this African moth is the most
beautiful of all living creatures. It lives on the
island of Madagascar, near the east coast of Africa.

A caterpillar community

It is one of the first warm days of early spring. There are no leaves on the trees yet. But many branches have tiny reddish or greenish buds. In a day or two, these will burst into little leaves.

Around a small branch on an apple tree, there is an odd, oblong swelling. It is a little more than half an inch (1.2 centimeters) long. It is brownish, like the tree's bark, and brittle, like dried glue.

This swelling isn't part of the tree. It was put on the branch last summer by a furry, brown female moth. Beneath it are the more than three hundred eggs she laid. As she laid them, a foamy stuff came out of her body. It covered the eggs and hardened into the brown swelling on the branch.

The eggs look like tiny, light-gray jars, tightly packed in rows. Their flat bottoms are glued to the branch. Inside each egg there is a tiny caterpillar. It is doubled up, like the letter U. Many of the caterpillars, using their strong, sharp jaws, are beginning to chew through the flat tops of their eggs.

One by one, each tiny caterpillar comes out of its egg. Then it chews its way through the brittle stuff covering the eggs. This brittle stuff is soon full of tiny holes. In a short time, hundreds of tiny caterpillars

are swarming on the covering. Their bodies are grayish-black, with gray bands. Long gray hairs stick out of their sides and backs.

Some of the caterpillars begin to explore. They crawl up toward the end of the branch. As they crawl, they lay down a trail of silk for their feet to cling to. Some of them drop off the branch. They dangle at the end of silk threads, as if trying to spy out the land. Soon, most of the little creatures have found leaf buds and are contentedly chewing.

When night comes, the caterpillars crawl back along their trails of silk. When they are together again, they spin a sort of silk carpet on the branch. Then they all nestle together in a thick clump of furry bodies.

During the night, the weather turns bitterly cold. A freezing rain begins to fall. The caterpillars lie stiff and motionless, frozen with cold.

A chilly day dawns. There are fewer caterpillars now. The rain has knocked some off the branch. Some have died from the cold. The others are still unable to move.

But the next day is sunny and warm. Many of the buds are now young leaves. Soon, the caterpillars are crawling away to eat.

For a few days, the caterpillars crawl about. Each one goes its own way. They are still exploring and finding out about the world they have come into. At night, by ones and twos, they come back to their gathering place.

Then, one day, some of the caterpillars begin to make a "tent." It is actually a silk web where two branches come together. The caterpillars move back and forth, "weaving" threads of silk together. Others join them. Soon, all are working. They make a small sheet of silk that covers the fork in the tree. From now on, this will be their home. And from now on, the caterpillars will do everything together.

At night, they all gather under the tent. In the morning, they all crawl up on top of it. Then, off they go, in several long lines. The caterpillar parades crawl along the tree trunk and out onto branches, toward the leaves.

For about two hours, the caterpillars eat. Then back they go to their tent. They crawl

about on it for a time, adding more silk to
it. Then, they all go inside for a "nap." Later
in the day, they all go back out onto the tent
roof to spin for a while. After that, they
parade off for a short lunch.

After lunch, it is time for another "nap."
This is followed by a great deal of eager
work on the tent. By then it is evening, and
the parades march off for a long, long
dinner that lasts until darkness. Everyone
returns to the tent for the night.

This is how the caterpillars spend each
day for the next five or six weeks. About
once a week they shed their skins and grow.
They always stay in the tent for a time

when they shed their skins. The tent is soon full of dried-up old skins!

The tent, too, grows. The caterpillars work on it every day. At the end of about six weeks it is a thick sheet of silk, a good two feet (60 cm) long.

During all this time, the caterpillars have done some damage to the tree. Each caterpillar eats about two leaves a day. So, together, they eat thousands of leaves. If there are five or six tent caterpillar nests on a small tree, the caterpillars can destroy the tree.

At the end of about forty days, the tent caterpillars are full grown. They are two inches (5 cm) long. Now their bodies are more colorful, with spots of blue and yellow, and a white stripe on the back.

And now their way of life changes. They spend the whole night eating and sleep all day. They stop working on the tent. It grows gray and tattered, like an old, ugly rag. The caterpillar community is coming to an end.

By ones and twos, the caterpillars leave the tree. They hurry along a branch until they reach the end. Then they flip themselves into the air and tumble to the ground!

Once on the ground, each caterpillar crawls off in a different direction. It seeks a hiding place, such as the underside of a fence rail or the bottom edge of a roof. The

place must be as far as possible from the tree where the caterpillar was hatched.

In its hiding place, the caterpillar doubles itself up and covers itself with a cocoon. As it spins silk around itself, most of its long hairs come off and are mixed in with the silk threads. The caterpillar squirts a yellow liquid into the cocoon. This makes the cocoon stiff and hard.

The change from caterpillar to moth takes about three weeks. When the moth is ready to leave the cocoon, a liquid oozes out of its mouth into the silk. The silk softens so that the moth can break through it.

The moth that wriggles out of the cocoon is a plain, brown creature. It really isn't very pretty. And it doesn't go about visiting flowers as butterflies and some moths do. It cannot eat! It has no jaws and no sipping tongue. Its stomach is too tiny to hold food.

The moth's only reason for living is to mate. After the females mate, they lay their three or four hundred eggs on a branch. Soon after, the grown-up moths die. But, next spring, many new tent caterpillars will hatch and everything will start over again.

a bagworm inside its tube

Caterpillars with mobile homes

Some kinds of moth caterpillars build homes for themselves. But these aren't ordinary homes—they are portable. The caterpillars carry them around!

These caterpillars are known as bagworms. As soon as a bagworm hatches, even before it begins to eat, it makes its home. It does this by spinning a tube of silk around itself. Mixed in with the silk are bits of leaves, twigs, and dirt. Then, with only its head and first six legs sticking out of the tube, the caterpillar crawls on its way.

The tube, or bag, is quite strong and tough. It protects the caterpillar. It looks just like a bit of dirt. Hungry birds pay no attention to it. When the caterpillar has to rest, or shed its skin, it uses sticky silk to fasten the tube to something. Then it pulls its whole body inside.

A bagworm never leaves its home until it becomes a moth. As the caterpillar grows, it simply makes the tube bigger. It changes from a caterpillar to a moth inside the tube.

Bagworm moths are quite tiny. Their wingspread is only about half an inch (12 millimeters). The caterpillars are tiny, too, of course. But they are big eaters. They often do a lot of damage to trees.

Disguises

A caterpillar climbs slowly up a branch. The caterpillar is long and slim. Its head is reddish and its body is pale green.

The caterpillar stops crawling. It has decided to rest. It grips the branch tightly with its back pair of legs. Then it swings its body away from the branch and holds itself stiff. Suddenly, it doesn't look like a caterpillar. Its body looks like a twig on the

clearwing butterfly
This butterfly lives in dim forests in Panama, where its transparent wings make it hard to see.

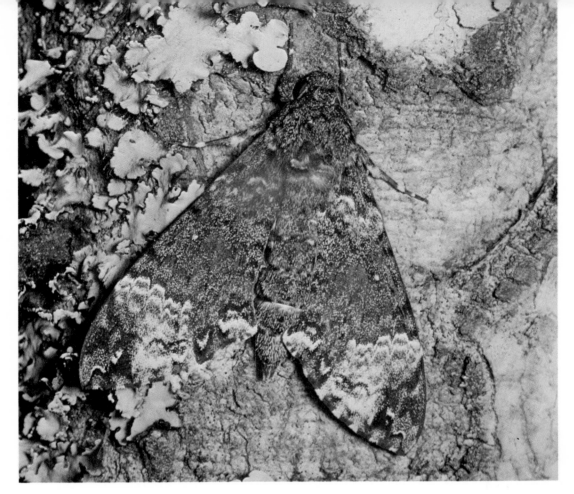

hawk moth

The colors on a hawk moth's wings make it blend into the bark when it rests on a tree.

branch. And its reddish head looks like a leaf bud.

A moth has been flying all night. Now, the sun is coming up. The moth will rest during the day.

The moth flies to a tree. It lays itself flat against the trunk, gripping the bark with the claws on its feet. The moth seems to vanish. Its speckled, brownish wings blend in perfectly with the bark on the tree.

Many kinds of caterpillars and moths can disguise themselves this way. Their bodies or wings are colored so that they blend in with leaves or bark, or look like a leaf or

twig. Sharp-eyed birds and other creatures that might eat the caterpillars and moths can't see them.

Some kinds of caterpillars have a different disguise. They are disguised to look like fierce hunting creatures. For example, the spicebush swallowtail caterpillar has two big spots of color high up on its back. The spots look like huge staring eyes. Many kinds of hunting creatures have large, bright eyes like this. So, it's likely that birds are frightened off by the sight of the caterpillar's "eyes" looking at them.

Some kinds of moths and butterflies also have these eye spots on their wings. When they open their wings, the "eyes" suddenly appear. This can so startle a bird, it leaves the moth or butterfly alone.

spicebush swallowtail caterpillar

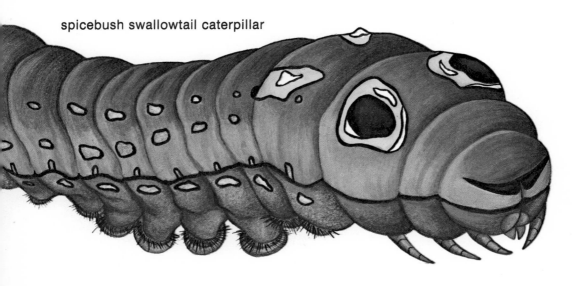

The Busy Workers

carpenter ant

Somebody up in the rocky pasture
   Heaved the stone over.
Here are the cells and a network of furrows
   In the roots of the clover.
Hundreds of eggs lie fitted in patterns,
   Waxy and yellow.
Hundreds of ants are racing and struggling.
   One little fellow
Shoulders an egg as big as his body,
   Ready for hatching.
Darkness is best, so everyone's rushing,
   Hastily snatching
Egg after egg to the lowest tunnels.
   And suddenly, where
Confusion had been, there is now nothing.
   Ants gone. Cells bare.

The Ant Village
Marion Edey and Dorothy Grider

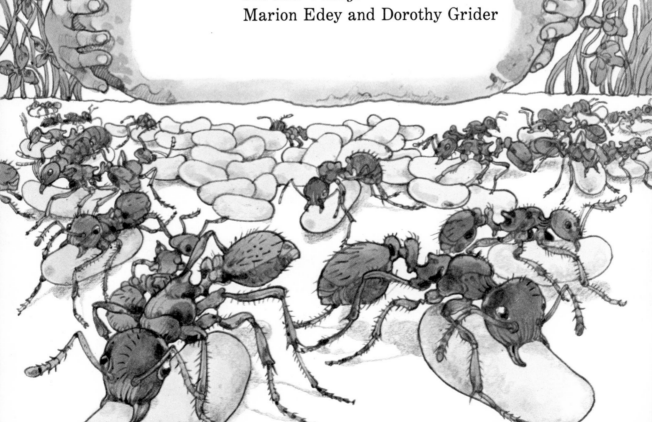

Ant babies

Sometime you may move a rock and find an ant nest. If you kneel down and watch for a while, you'll see an amazing sight. The ants rush about so fast their legs seem to twinkle. Each ant picks up what looks like a white egg and carries it out of sight. In a short time, just as the poem says, there isn't an ant or a white object in sight!

Actually, the white or yellowish objects aren't eggs. Ant eggs are tiny specks. These objects are really baby ants. They are either ant larvae—wormlike babies—or pupae— baby ants in cocoons.

Baby ants have no eyes or legs. They are fed, cared for, and moved about by grown-up ants. These ant "nurses" spend a lot of time licking the babies. This keeps the babies clean. The grown-up ants don't know this, of course. They simply lick the babies because the babies taste good! They taste good because little drops of sweet liquid ooze out of an ant larva's body.

When most kinds of ant larvae are ready to become adults, they spin a silk cocoon around themselves, just as many kinds of caterpillars do. The cocoon is oblong and yellowish-white. When the new adult is ready to come out of its cocoon, an ant "nurse" often helps it.

Life in an ant nest

A female ant comes skimming out of the sky on long, rounded wings. Her black body shines in the warm summer sunlight. She lands gently in a broad meadow.

She started out in the morning, from a nest several miles away—the nest where she was born. She will never see it again. Now she is going to start her own nest. She will be the queen and the mother. All the ants in the nest will be her children. While she was flying, she mated with several winged male ants from the old nest. Eggs are now growing in her body.

She begins to wiggle and rub herself against the ground. After a time, one of her wings comes off. She wiggles and rubs until the other wing breaks loose. She will never need wings again.

She begins to explore, trotting between the grass stems that rise like tall trees around her. Coming to a small, bare patch of sandy earth, she stops. Using her jaws and front feet, she begins to dig. Soon, she has made a hole big enough to lie in.

Now she lies in the hole and waits. Many months go by—nearly a year. In all that time, the young queen never eats. She gets her food from her body fat and the two big muscles on her back, where her wings were attached. These muscles slowly shrink as

her body turns them into food to keep her alive.

At last, the queen begins to lay some eggs. She now needs food badly—so she eats some of the eggs. Baby ants hatch from the others. The queen feeds them with a liquid that comes from inside her body.

After a time, the babies spin cocoons around themselves and change into adults. They are all females. But they have no wings, and they will never be able to lay eggs. They are not queens like their mother. They are workers—the first workers in the new nest.

The queen soon lays more eggs. Babies hatch out. These babies are fed by the first workers. In time, the babies become adult workers, too. They are bigger and stronger than the first workers.

The tiny nest begins to grow. The workers dig tunnels and passageways in several directions. They make special rooms to keep the larvae in. The ants dig by grabbing bits of earth with their jaws and carrying the dirt up out of the nest. Then they go back for another bit. Back and forth, and in and out, they go. They do this again and again, until the tunnel or room is finished.

While some workers dig, others care for the larvae. They lick them, feed them, and move them about to keep them cool. Still other workers scurry out of the nest in

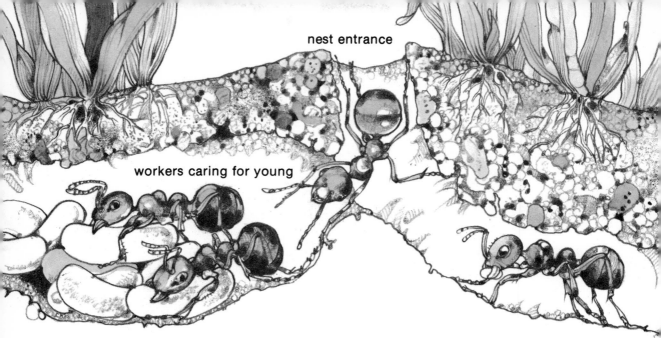

nest entrance

workers caring for young

search of food, or scurry into the nest, bringing in food. An ant worker is always doing some job!

No one "tells" the workers what to do. But there are always a few workers that start doing things, and this causes other workers to join in. One or two workers may begin digging and others will quickly come to help. Or, a worker may start to move larvae to a cooler place. Then others will rush to take up the task, too.

When an ant that is exploring outside the nest finds food, she hurries back to the nest. Soon, many ants stream out of the nest, straight for the food. The worker that found the food hasn't actually "told" the others where to find it. When she returns to the nest with a bit of food, she leaves a trail of scent. The smell causes other workers to

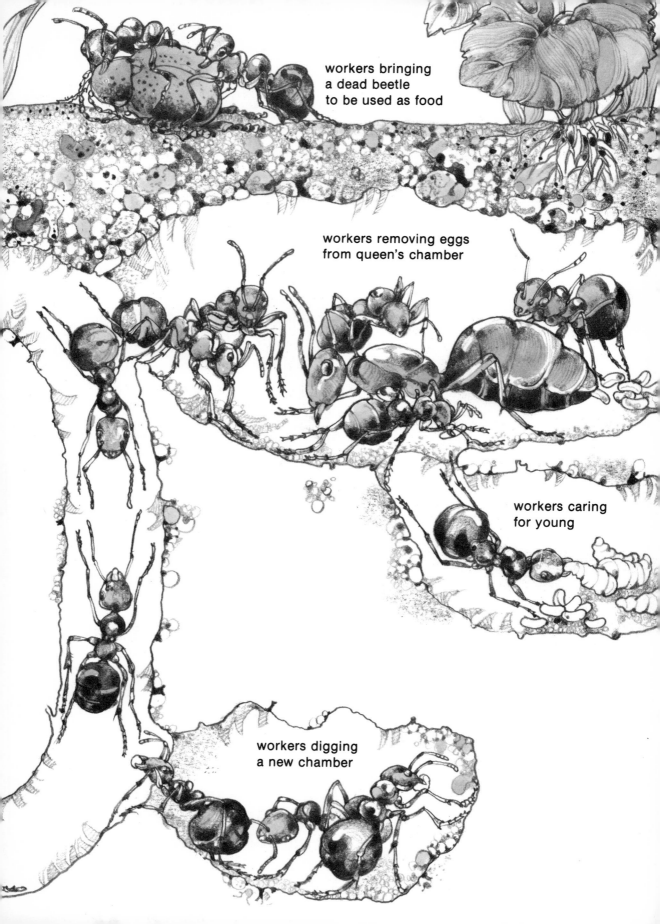

workers bringing
a dead beetle
to be used as food

workers removing eggs
from queen's chamber

workers caring
for young

workers digging
a new chamber

want to find food, too. All they have to do is follow the scent trail made by the first ant.

Smell is tremendously important to the ants. Every ant in the nest has the same smell, so every ant with that smell is a "friend." When a worker enters the nest with food, all the others know she belongs there. If another worker "asks" her for some food, she can tell by smell that the other is a friend. Then she'll put some of the food she carries in her mouth into the other's mouth. But any ant or other insect with a different smell is an enemy. It will be driven away if it tries to enter the nest.

All summer long the nest is a busy, active place. But in the wintertime it is still and silent. The ants lie motionless in the cold darkness. They are alive, but their bodies are too stiff to move. They are in a kind of "frozen" sleep. In the spring, the sun warms them and they are able to move again. Once more, the ant colony bustles with activity.

Several years pass. Then, a very special day comes. Some of the queen's young have become winged females, as she once was. Others have become winged males. The time has come for these ants to leave the nest.

It is like an ant holiday! As the males and females walk out of the nest, the excited workers swarm around them. One by one, the females and males soar into the air. There, they will mate. Then the females will

land far away and start new nests. Thus, every ant nest is begun by an ant that has come from somewhere else.

Life in the old nest goes on for many more years. But one day the queen dies. The ant colony is doomed. No more eggs are laid. The workers die. The once bustling colony is empty and lifeless—like the ruin of an ancient city.

There are many different kinds of ants. They don't all live in the same way. Some ants make their nests in plants, or out of leaves. Some do not have any nest. They simply move about from place to place. Some queens don't start their own nest— they move into an old nest, murder its queen, and take over. And some nests have more than one queen.

But, all ants live in communities. There are no "hermits" in the ant world.

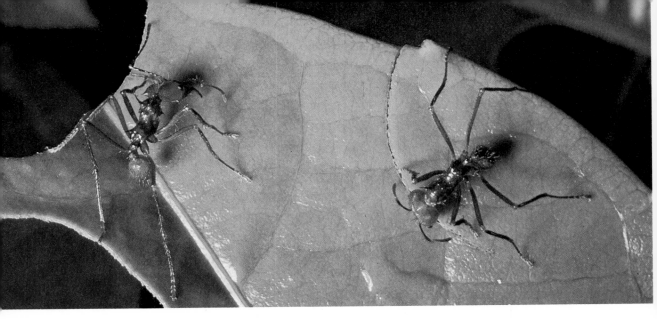

leaf-cutter ants

Leaf-cutter ants use their jaws to cut curved pieces out of leaves. They use the bits of leaf as fertilizer for their underground "gardens."

Farmer ants

Scurrying through the grass is what looks like a parade of ants. They trot one after the other, in a long line. Each ant carries a large piece of leaf above its head, like a green umbrella!

The ant parade goes into an underground nest. The nest is wide and deep, for it is the home of almost a million ants. There are many tunnels and rooms. Some go down as much as sixteen and a half feet (5 meters) into the ground. The nest has a thousand entrances.

The ants hurry down long, winding tunnels until they come to a large room. In this room are a number of whitish, furry-looking patches. These are about as big as the palm of your hand. The patches are the ants' farms. For these ants are farmers—*true* farmers. They grow their

own food in "fields" that they water, fertilize, and weed!

These farmer ants are known as leaf-cutter ants. That's because they use their sharp jaws to cut bits of leaves or flowers. They carry these pieces into their nest, to use as fertilizer for their fields.

The ants' crop is a fungus—a kind of plant that is like a mushroom, or like the mold that grows on bread. The fungus grows on a stalk with a knob on the end. These knobs are the ants' food.

Fungus can grow in the underground darkness as long as it has water and food— which the ants give it. The ants chew the bits of leaves and flowers into a soft, wet pulp. They put this pulp on the fields of fungus. In this way, they keep the fungus watered and fertilized.

This one kind of fungus is the leaf-cutter ants' only food. They could not live without it. And it could not grow without the care and help the ants give it.

When a young leaf-cutter queen flies off to start a new nest she carries with her a tiny bit of fungus from the old nest. When she digs the first part of the new nest, she starts a new farm with the fungus. She takes care of it herself, until the first of her children are able to do this. Without a healthy, growing fungus farm, the new nest would be doomed.

Ants that keep "cows"

In many parts of the world, people keep herds of cows or sheep for the milk they give. And there are some kinds of ants that keep herds of little insects called aphids, for a sweet drink the aphids give!

Aphids live on plants and are often called "plant lice." They suck the sugary juice that's in the leaves, stems, and roots of plants. A lot of the juice they eat simply goes right through them and drips out of their bodies.

Many kinds of ants love this sweet juice. They run about on leaves, licking up drops of the juice that aphids leave behind. Often, an ant will "milk" an aphid, much as a person milks a cow. The ant does this by rubbing its feelers against the aphid's body. Then the aphid lets a drop of the sweet juice, called honeydew, ooze out of its body for the ant to lick up.

For some kinds of ants, aphid honeydew is the main food. These ants really do protect and take care of aphids, much as people look after herds of cows! This is why they are called dairying ants.

One kind of dairying ant lives in cornfields in parts of the United States and Canada. Their aphids feed on the roots of corn plants. In the fall, when the aphids lay eggs, the ants gather up the eggs. They

carry the eggs into their underground nest to protect them during winter.

In the spring, the ants bring out the eggs to hatch. When the eggs hatch, the ants carry the young aphids to the roots of young corn plants. The aphids feed on the roots and make honeydew. This is fine for the ants, but it kills the corn.

When a young queen ant flies off to begin a new colony, she carries with her a mother aphid that's ready to lay eggs. Thus, when the queen starts her colony, her ants will have their own herd of aphids!

hunter ants

These African hunter ants attacked a termite and tore it to pieces with their sharp, curved jaws.

Hunter ants

Many kinds of ants eat almost anything they can find—seeds, honeydew, spilled human food, dead insects. Sometimes, these ants also hunt. Several of them may attack a beetle or other insect, and kill it. Then they drag it back to the nest, for food.

Other kinds of ants live only by hunting. They eat only the fresh "meat" of insects, spiders, and other creatures they hunt and kill. These fierce hunter ants usually have long, strong jaws, often with many sharp teeth on them. And they have stingers that can kill an insect, and even cause pain to a person.

Even the babies are meat-eaters! The hunters bring back the insects they've killed, tear them up, and throw the pieces to

bulldog ant
Australian bulldog ants are
fierce hunters. They have
tiny sharp teeth on their
long, pointed jaws.

the babies. Then the babies scramble and
fight to get their share. In fact, if the babies
are hungry enough, some may even try to
eat one of the others!

Hunter ants live together in nests, as
other ants do. But they seldom go hunting
together. Each hunter is on its own. Even
the queen does her own hunting.

Some of the biggest and fiercest hunting
ants live in Australia. They are known as
"bulldog ants" and "jumpers." These ants
are as much as an inch (2.5 centimeters)
long. They will even attack people who come
too near their nest—and their sting is very
painful!

The biggest of all ants is a hunting ant
more than an inch (2.5 cm) long. These
giant ants live in colonies of a hundred or so
in the forests of South America.

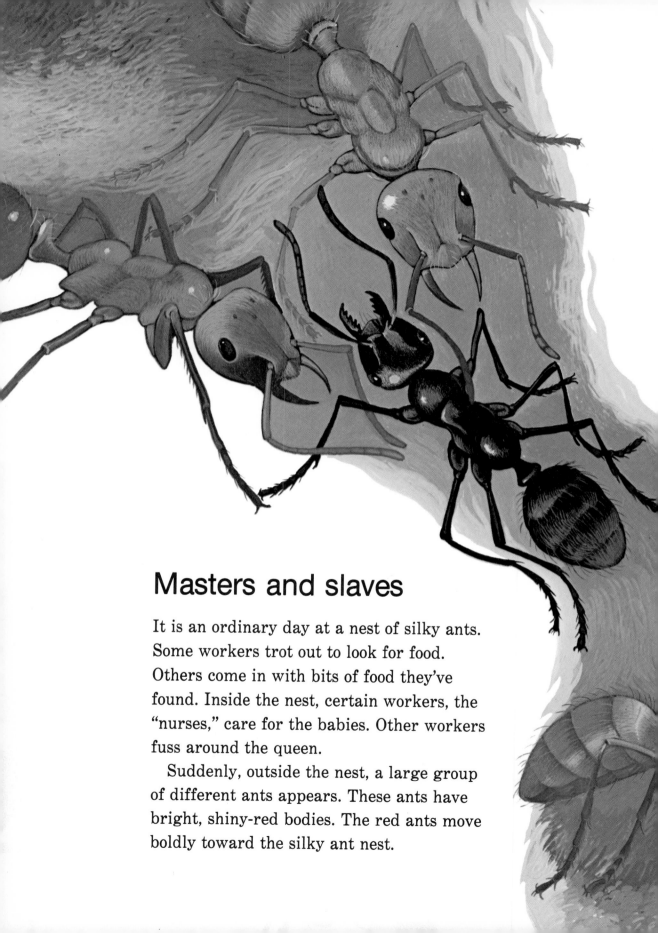

Masters and slaves

It is an ordinary day at a nest of silky ants.
Some workers trot out to look for food.
Others come in with bits of food they've
found. Inside the nest, certain workers, the
"nurses," care for the babies. Other workers
fuss around the queen.

Suddenly, outside the nest, a large group
of different ants appears. These ants have
bright, shiny-red bodies. The red ants move
boldly toward the silky ant nest.

It is an attacking army! The attackers swarm into the nest. The silky ants fight to defend their home. But they cannot beat the red ants. The long, curved jaws of the red ants are terrible weapons.

The red ants charge through the tunnels. Killing any "nurse" that tries to stop them, they seize the baby silky ants. Then they rush back through the tunnels, out of the nest. Carrying the captured larvae, the red ants hurry back to their own nest.

Why did the red ants steal the silky ant babies? What are they going to do with

them? The silky ant babies are going to become "slaves" of the red ants!

The red ants have big, sharp jaws and are fierce fighters—but fighting is the only thing they can do. They can't even feed themselves without help! So, they must have "slaves." This is why they raid the nests of silky ants and carry off the young. When the young silky ants become adults, they do all the work of getting food, caring for the young, and looking after the red ants.

When a red queen starts a new nest, she doesn't begin digging, as most young ant queens do. She simply looks for a nest of silky ants and marches into it. When she finds the queen, she murders her and becomes the new queen of the nest!

The silky ants treat the red ant just as they treated their own queen. When she starts laying eggs, they care for the eggs just as they would care for their own eggs. They treat the red ants that hatch out just as they treat each other.

In time, of course, there are fewer silky ants, because none of their kind of eggs are being laid. That's when the red ants begin to raid other silky ant nests, to capture more "slaves."

So, a red ant nest is home to two different kinds of ants—red ants who can't do anything but fight, and silky ants who do all the work.

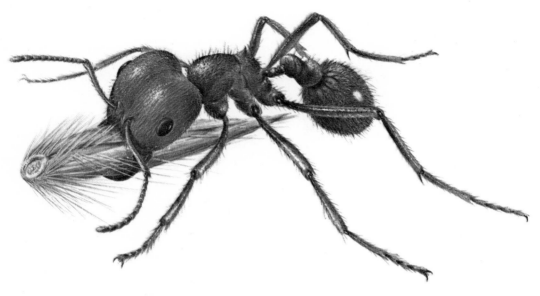

Harvester ants

Harvesters are people who gather up the ripe crops in late summer and fall. Some kinds of ants are known as harvesters. When the seeds of many plants grow ripe and plump, the ants gather them up and bring them into the nest. The ants eat some of the seeds right away. But they also store seeds in the nest. This way they always have food when they can't find fresh seeds.

Most seeds the ants bring into the nest are still in their husks, or shells. The ants take the seeds out of the husks and store them. Then they carry the husks up out of the nest and throw them away. You can often tell where a harvester ant nest is by the wide ring of seed husks lying all around it.

Sometimes the stored seeds get damp. Then workers will carry them all outside and put them in the sunshine to dry.

honeypot ants

Some honeypot ant workers, like the one on the right, stuff themselves with honey until their bodies are round. Then they hang from the ceiling of the nest (above), as living honey jars for the other ants.

Honeypot ants

If you could walk into a nest of the ants known as honeypots, you would see a strange sight. There would be many large, round, glistening balls hanging from the ceiling in many of the rooms. And, after a moment, you would see that these balls are *alive*. They are ants whose stomachs are swollen up to the size of a marble. These ants are the nest's *live* honeypots!

The workers in a honeypot nest collect sweet honeydew from plants and from aphids. They store the honeydew in their throats. When they have enough, they hurry back to the nest. Then they squirt the liquid into the mouths of certain workers.

Soon, these workers have swallowed so much honeydew their stomachs swell up. They can hardly move. They crawl up onto the ceiling of a room and hang there. The workers that collect the honeydew keep squirting it into the mouths of these hanging ants. These honeypots are living storage tanks for the colony's food.

When a worker is hungry, she goes to a honeypot and taps it with her antennae. The honeypot then squirts some of the honeydew from its stomach into her mouth! Thus, the workers always have a ready supply of food.

154

tailor ants

Some kinds of ants live in trees. They make nests (right) out of leaves. Some of the ants pull the edges of a leaf together. Others "glue" the edges together (below) with sticky silk made by babies the workers carry in their jaws.

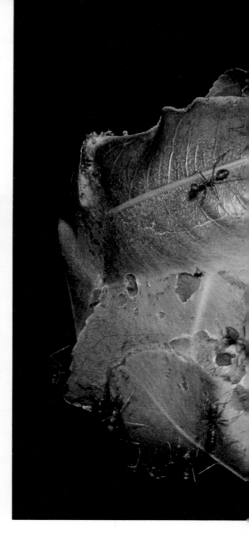

Living "glue tubes"

In several places around the world there are ants that make nests by gluing leaves together. To do this, they use living "glue tubes!"

These ants live in trees. To make a new nest, a number of ants pull the edges of two leaves together. If the leaves are far apart, the ants form a chain to reach from one leaf to another. One ant holds another by the waist, and so on, until finally an ant at the

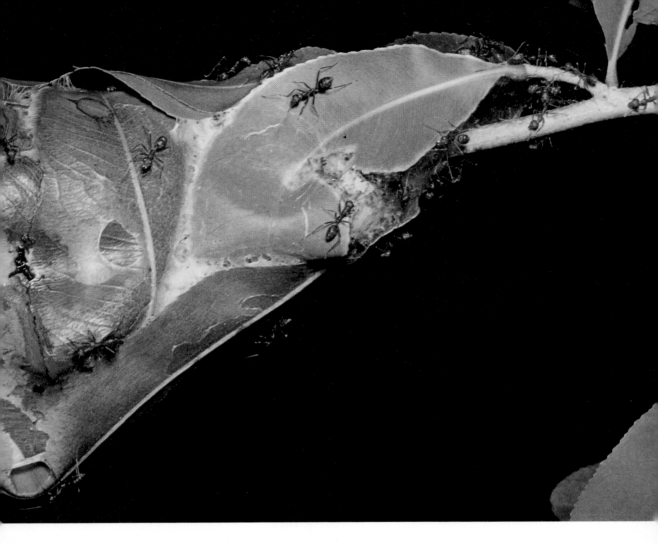

end of a chain can grab the leaf. Then the
ants in the chain work their way backwards
until the leaves are pulled together!

When the leaves are together, other ants
bring the "glue tubes"—which are baby
ants! Each ant carries a baby, or larva,
which can ooze sticky silk from its head.
The ants rub the larvae back and forth over
the edges of the leaves to glue them
together!

A colony of these ants may have a number
of leaf-nests hanging in several trees.

A conquering army

A raiding army is moving through a forest. Every living creature in its path is in deadly danger. The soldiers of this army will kill any creature that can't get away!

By the tens of thousands, the soldiers swarm among the trees. There are so many of them they hide the ground. Their weapons are their jaws, which are like curved, sharp swords. These soldiers are ants, and they are seeking food.

A dozen of the soldiers come upon a beetle larva. In an instant, it is torn to bits. Other soldiers find a sick armadillo that can't move. It is hundreds of times bigger than

an ant, but the ants swarm over it by the thousands. It, too, is cut to pieces. Any animal that can't get out of the path of the raiders is doomed. Even a large animal, such as a cow, can be chewed to bits until only the bones are left!

Army ants, as this kind of ant is called, do not have a regular nest. Every so often, army ants "make camp," perhaps beneath the roots of a tree. There, they huddle in a huge, glistening cluster. For about nine days, the queen lays eggs—thousands of them. Meanwhile, thousands of baby ants lie wrapped in cocoons, changing into adults.

After another ten days, the eggs have hatched. At the same time, the babies that

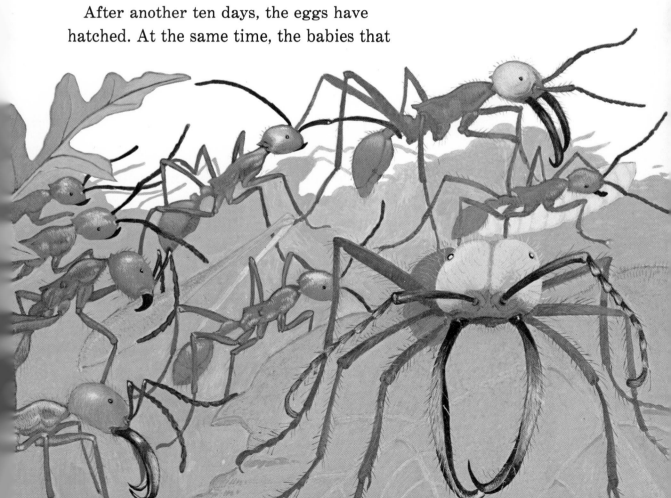

have now become adults begin to break out of their cocoons. Both the babies and the new adults are fiercely hungry—and they must have meat! So, the army moves off in search of food.

The horde of ants moves mostly by night. The babies are carried by workers. The big-headed, sharp-jawed soldiers move at the front and sides of the army. The queen marches along near the rear. She is bigger than all the other ants, and is always surrounded by a crowd of workers.

This army of ants cannot see where it is going. Most kinds of army ants are blind. However, as each ant moves it leaves a scent trail behind it. So, each ant simply follows the trail of the ants ahead. The ants at the front have no trail to follow, of course. They just move forward blindly, pushed along by those behind them.

The army halts by day. This is when the swarms or columns of raiders move out in search of food. Every insect, spider, worm, animal, or bird the soldiers run into is attacked at once. Many creatures are eaten on the spot. Others are torn to bits and the pieces carried back to the rest of the army.

After about three weeks, most of the army is well fed. The babies are beginning to spin cocoons around themselves. So, once again the army halts and "makes camp." Once again, the queen begins to lay eggs.

Guests and pests

You'd be horrified if your family invited guests into your home—and let the guests eat you! But that's what some ants do!

In many ant nests there are often a number of little beetles. The beetles can make a liquid ooze out of a place on their back. The ants love this liquid. An ant will often stroke a beetle, which then makes a drop of the liquid for the ant to lick up. So the ants are "glad" to have the beetles staying in the nest. Whenever a beetle goes to an ant for food, the ant feeds it.

However, some of the beetles aren't always satisfied with plain ant food. Sometimes they eat ant eggs and ant babies! And the ants let them do it! It seems that as long as the beetles supply their sweet liquid, the ants let them do what they please!

There are often many different creatures in an ant nest. But they're not all welcome guests like the beetles. Many of them are pests and thieves.

Some of these pests are mites. Mites are tiny, eight-legged creatures related to spiders. A mite will fasten itself onto an ant, usually close to the ant's head. The ant can't get the mite off, so it has to carry the mite everywhere. Whenever the ant gives food to or gets food from another ant—the mite reaches out and steals some!

ant feeding a beetle

The wood eaters

In an old house, some of the wooden boards begin to crumble away. An old, dead tree suddenly splits and crashes to the ground. A thick piece of timber supporting a bridge suddenly gives way and the bridge collapses. When such things happen, chances are that termites have been at work!

Termites are insects that eat wood. In North America, communities of termites live in dead trees and in the wooden parts of houses. The termites eat many long, branching tunnels in the wood around their nest. In time, the wood becomes almost hollow. What looks like a solid tree or board may be as thin as paper!

Strangely, although termites eat wood, they can't digest it as we digest our food. Tiny, one-celled creatures that live in the termites' stomachs do this for them.

Termites are often called "white ants," but they aren't even closely related to ants. They're more like cockroaches. However, like ants, they live in communities.

At certain times, swarms of winged male and female termites fly from an old nest. When a male and female find one another, they dig a small, hidden nest.

After a time, the female lays her first eggs. The babies that hatch have six legs

and can run about. These baby termites don't spin cocoons to become adults. They simply keep growing and shedding their skins. In time, most become adult workers or soldiers. Some become winged adults.

The termite workers are small and have soft, pale bodies. Their small jaws are good only for digging or carrying things. But the soldiers are big, with large, hard heads and long, sharp jaws that are deadly weapons. Some kinds of termites have both workers and soldiers in the nest, but some kinds have only soldiers.

Most kinds of termite workers and soldiers are blind. But they don't really need eyes. Most of them never leave the nest, which is completely dark.

termites

Many kinds of termites make nests in wood, which they eat. The smaller termite (left) is a worker, the other is a soldier.

termite mound

This huge mound was built by tiny African termites. Their nest is inside the mound.

A termite city

On the plains of East Africa there are many strange reddish towers. These towers rise as much as twenty feet (6 meters) high. They look a bit like lumpy pyramids. If you were to touch one, you would find it is as hard as rock. These strange towers are termite nests.

An African termite tower is an amazing place. It is home for nearly a million termites. Each tower is a sealed-up "city" of many tunnels and rooms. There is even a great "garden," for these termites are "farmers" and raise most of their own food. This food is a simple plant, called fungus, that can grow in the dark.

The termite city is ruled by a queen and a king. It is guarded by an army of fierce soldiers. And it is kept running by a host of busy, active workers.

The workers do all kinds of tasks. They dig new tunnels. They build new walls with sand and clay brought up from below the ground. They tend the mold gardens, where the city's food is grown. They feed the queen, king, babies, and soldiers. They take care of the queen's eggs.

The soldiers don't do anything but fight. So, most of the time they have nothing to do. They usually just wander around the nest, begging for food. Because the soldiers aren't able to feed themselves, the workers have to feed them. Sometimes, if a nest has too many soldiers and not enough food, some of the soldiers are put to death! They are simply starved to death—no worker will give them any food.

But there are times when the soldiers are needed. The termites have a bitter enemy—ants! At times, ants from a nearby nest, or

perhaps a horde of army ants, will break
into the tower. Then the termite soldiers
rush into battle. They will fight to the death
to drive off the invaders.

The termite queen does nothing but lay
eggs. She may lay as many as forty
thousand eggs a day! In order to lay so
many eggs, she has to eat almost all the
time. So she grows big and fat! Some kinds
of termite queens grow to look like a small
sausage, as much as five inches (12.5
centimeters) long and an inch (2.5 cm) wide.
Such a queen is more than two thousand
times bigger than a tiny worker. She is so
heavy she can't move.

A swarm of workers always surrounds the
queen. They bring her food and lick her
body. And there is always a crowd of other
termites moving in and out of her chamber.

termite queen and workers

A termite queen does nothing but lay eggs. Workers feed her. She becomes as large and fat as a small sausage.

There are even "police" termites on hand, to keep the crowd from getting too close to the queen! It is almost as if the queen's subjects want to be near her, just as people often want to be near some famous or important person.

As long as the queen lays eggs, she is the most important termite in the nest. But if she stops, she is doomed. The workers stop giving her food. After she starves to death, they eat her! A young female termite is then chosen as the new queen. She mates with the old king, and starts laying eggs.

All this happens in complete darkness. Termites dislike light, and most of them never leave the nest. Sometimes, workers must go outside to find new soil for the mold garden. Then, they build long tunnels of mud to protect themselves from sunlight.

The Honey Makers

honeybee

How doth the little busy bee
  Improve each shining hour
And gather honey all the day
  From every passing flower!

How skilfully she builds her cell;
  How neat she spreads the wax!
And labours hard to store it well
  With the sweet food she makes.
How Doth the Little Busy Bee
Isaac Watts

The way
of the honeybee

It is springtime, and an apple tree has burst into bloom. Its blossoms are puffs of white against bright-green leaves. But a honeybee buzzing about nearby sees the blossoms as bright blue-green spots against a background of yellow leaves! The color and smell of the blossoms are a signal to the bee. This is how she knows the tree has something for her.

She alights on one of the blossoms and pushes down into it. Stretching out her tongue, which is like a long tube, she sucks up the bit of sweet nectar inside the flower. She flits from one blossom to another, sucking up more nectar. Soon, the little sack, or honey stomach, inside her body is full.

All the time the bee is getting the nectar, she is also doing something important for the tree. As she pushes into each flower, she gets a yellowish powder, called pollen, all over her hairy body. Some of this pollen rubs off in each flower she visits. Pollen from one flower makes seeds start to grow in another flower. In this way, the bee helps the flowers make seeds from which new apple trees will grow.

The bee also collects some of the pollen for

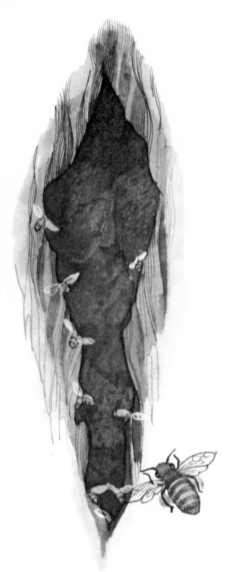

food. She scrapes some of it off herself and mixes it with a tiny bit of nectar, to make sticky lumps. She pushes these golden lumps into "baskets" of stiff hairs on her back legs.

When her "baskets" and honey stomach are full, the bee no longer flies here and there in search of flowers, as before. Now, she heads straight home, making a beeline for her hive. The hive, which is in a hollow tree, is home for some fifty thousand bees. Most of them are workers. But there is one queen bee. She does nothing but lay eggs.

All workers are females. These workers search for food, keep the hive clean, care for the young, and guard the entrance to the hive. To protect herself and defend the hive, each worker has a stinger on her tail. It is

like a spearpoint with hooks on it. When a worker stings a creature, the hooks catch in the creature's body and the stinger is pulled out of the bee. A worker bee dies a few hours after she loses her stinger.

Reaching the hollow tree, the bee goes past some guard bees and through a large crack in the trunk. Hanging down inside the tree are a number of long, thick strips of wax. These are the honeycombs. Each comb is made up of thousands of tiny "rooms," or cells, all joined together. Thousands of workers built these combs out of bits of wax that came from their bodies.

The six-sided cells are storerooms. Many are filled with honey or with pollen—food for the bees. In some cells there are long, slim eggs. In others, there are little, wormlike baby bees. Still other cells are covered with wax lids. In these cells lie baby bees wrapped in silk cocoons. These babies are changing into adults.

The bee that found the apple tree alights on part of a comb that has many empty cells. At once, she is surrounded by other workers. Several stretch out their tongues to her. She brings up nectar from her honey stomach. Each one sucks up some of it. But they don't eat it. One worker scurries off to feed the nectar to a baby bee. Others put their nectar into empty cells. In a few days, it will thicken into honey.

honey
in cells

workers sharing nectar

larvae

queen surrounded
by workers

wax-covered cells

young queen's cell

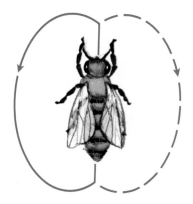

the bee dance

When a bee finds a place to get nectar, she flies straight home. In the nest, she does a "dance" that shows other bees how to find the nectar. She trots in straight lines and scurries in circles. The straight lines show the direction to take. The circles show the distance to the nectar.

Meanwhile, the bee that brought the nectar begins an odd sort of "dance." She does her "dance" over and over again, while the other workers swarm excitedly around her. She is showing them where the apple tree is. Each time she makes a straight line, she is pointing the direction to the tree. And the way she makes circles shows the distance to the tree.

Soon, many workers are winging toward the apple tree. Some fill themselves with nectar. Others collect only pollen. When the "baskets" on their legs are filled, these bees fly back to the hive. There, they scrape the pollen into empty cells in the honeycombs.

When a cell is filled, other workers take over. They let wax ooze out of their bodies. They chew it until it is soft and then use it to make wax covers for all of the pollen-filled cells.

Workers hatch from most of the queen's eggs. But a few baby queens hatch. And some males hatch. Soon, these babies start to spin cocoons around themselves. This seems to be a signal. Suddenly, the queen and many of the workers rush out of the hive! They fly away in a great swarm. They will start a new hive somewhere else. Never again will they return to the hollow tree.

About half the workers are left behind. They go about their work as usual. But now there is no queen.

In a few days, one of the young queens becomes an adult and breaks out of her cocoon. She searches for every cell in which there is another young queen in a cocoon. One by one, she kills all the others! She is the hollow tree's new queen, and she wants no rivals! She does her killing with her smooth, curved stinger, which is used only to kill other queens. Unlike a worker, a queen does not lose her stinger when she uses it. Nor does she die afterward.

The males, or drones, are also adults now. They don't do any work. They have no stinger. Their only purpose in life is to mate with a young queen.

After a few days, the queen and all the drones leave the hive. As the drones follow, the queen flies higher and higher. Finally, one drone reaches her, and they mate. Then, the drone dies. The queen and the other drones return to the hive. After a time, the queen begins to lay eggs.

Spring turns into summer. Each day, the busy worker bees search the land around the hollow tree for nectar and pollen. Some of this is eaten by the workers or fed to the larvae, the queen, and the drones. But a lot of the nectar is stored away as food for the winter.

Young workers do most of the work inside the hive. The youngest spend their time cleaning out pits, so that the queen can lay

a new queen bee

A baby queen bee changes into an adult in a cell shaped a bit like a peanut. The first queen to break out of her cell becomes the hive's new queen.

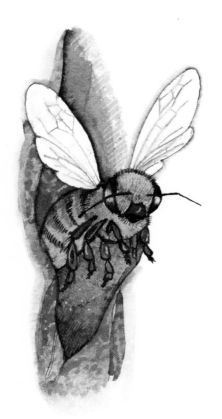

eggs in them. Young workers also feed the babies. As a worker grows older, she becomes a builder, making and repairing combs with the wax from her body. The oldest workers hunt for food. During the summer, a worker lives only about six weeks after becoming an adult.

In autumn, the bees begin to get ready for winter. One of the first things they do is to push all the drones out of the hive. The drones are left to starve to death because they are of no use now.

The queen lays fewer and fewer eggs. Finally, she lays no eggs at all. As the inside of the nest grows colder, the workers bunch together on both sides of a honey-filled comb. They form a big crowd, with the queen in the middle.

All winter long, the bees stay pressed together. But they keep moving and wiggling their wings. From time to time, they take sips of honey to keep up their energy. The heat of their bodies and their movements keep them fairly warm. Most of them live through the winter. And when spring comes, the life of the hive will start up again.

Bumblebees

Bumblebees are usually bigger and sturdier than honeybees. They live in an underground nest, which is often in an old mousehole. Like honeybees, they collect nectar and make honey. But they don't store the honey in wax combs. They save their old cocoons and store their honey in them.

A bumblebee queen starts a nest by herself in the spring. She makes a tiny "pot" out of wax from her body. Into this, she puts a ball of pollen and nectar. She lays eggs on the pollen ball. When the baby bees hatch, they're lying on their food.

The queen lays eggs during the summer. Most of the babies become workers and gather food. But not much food is needed. At summer's end, all the bees die.

During late summer, young queens and males hatch from some of the eggs. They fly off and mate. In winter, young bumblebee queens hide in the ground. In the spring, they come out and life starts again.

Unlike honeybees, bumblebees do not lose their stinger or die after using it. Bumblebees can sting again and again.

bumblebee nest
The yellowish balls are cocoons. After the young bees come out of them, workers use the empty cocoons for storing honey and pollen.

Solitary bees

There are several thousand kinds of bees other than honeybees and bumblebees. Most of these bees are known as solitary bees. *Solitary* means "alone." These bees are called solitary bees because they don't live together in communities, as do honeybees and bumblebees.

The solitary bees called carpenter bees

carpenter bee

A mother carpenter bee makes little "rooms" in a branch. In each room she puts a ball of pollen and nectar, on which she lays an egg. The babies then hatch right on top of the food they need.

make their nests in tree branches, stumps, or wooden posts. A mother carpenter bee digs out a short tunnel. Then she divides it into rooms with walls made of wood chips. In each room she puts some pollen mixed with nectar, and lays an egg. When a baby hatches, all the food it needs is in its room.

The mother stays in the last room she makes. When the babies become adults, they leave their rooms and join her. Then, they all fly away together.

Leaf-cutting bees also make their nests in dry branches or posts. But they make the rooms out of curved pieces of leaves. They use their sharp jaws as scissors to cut the leaves. If you ever see a leaf that has curved pieces missing, you'll know a leaf-cutting bee has been at work.

Mining bees make their nests underground. They dig a long tunnel, with smaller tunnels branching out from it. At the end of each small tunnel they put some food and lay an egg. Then they block up the tunnel.

One kind of solitary bee, called a mason bee, makes nests in empty snail shells! The mother bee puts a lump of pollen mixed with nectar into the shell and lays an egg on it. To protect the egg, she blocks off the opening of the shell with bits of leaves and tiny stones. Then she covers the shell with dried grass so it can't be seen.

Hunters
and
Builders

wasp

When the ripe pears droop heavily,
  The yellow wasp hums loud and long
  His hot and drowsy autumn song:
A yellow flame he seems to be,
  When darting suddenly from high
  He lights where fallen peaches lie.

Yellow and black—this tiny thing's
A tiger-soul on elfin wings.
                The Wasp
                by William Sharp

The hunting wasp

The female wasp buzzing among the flowers seemed quite harmless. She spent her days sipping nectar from flowers and basking in the sunshine. Caterpillars and other insects crawled about, but she paid no attention to them. She wasn't a meat-eater.

One day she began to dig in the ground. She dug with her jaws, lifting up bits of dirt and putting them in a pile. She worked slowly and carefully. After several hours, her work was finished. She had made a short tunnel with a round room at the end.

Picking up a clump of dirt, she sealed off the entrance to the tunnel. Carefully, she smoothed out the dirt around the entrance. She wanted to hide all signs of her work so that no other creature could find the nest.

When the nest was completely hidden, the wasp rose into the air. Several times she circled over the place. She picked out landmarks to remember, so that she could find the nest again.

Then she sped away on humming wings. Now she was no longer harmless—she had become a hunter, seeking her prey! She was ready to lay eggs. And though she did not eat meat, her babies would. She was hunting food for them.

She passed over a bumblebee busy getting nectar from a flower. It wasn't the kind of

creature she wanted. She skimmed above a grasshopper, but she didn't want it, either.

Then she saw a large caterpillar crawling on a leaf. This was her prey!

She swooped onto the caterpillar's back. At once, it began to jerk and hump its back, like a wild horse trying to throw off a rider. But the wasp clamped her jaws to the caterpillar's head and hung on tightly. The long, sharp stinger in her tail stabbed down into the caterpillar's body. The caterpillar stopped moving.

The caterpillar wasn't dead. The poison from the wasp's stinger hadn't killed it. But the caterpillar was paralyzed and could not move. The wasp stung the caterpillar several more times. Now the caterpillar would not be able to move for a long time.

The wasp began to drag the caterpillar back to the nest she had dug. It was hard

work. The caterpillar was bigger and heavier than she. But, finally, she reached the nest.

It took the wasp a few moments to find the hidden entrance to the nest. Quickly, she dug it open. Grabbing the caterpillar's head in her jaws, she dragged the caterpillar into the room at the end of the tunnel. She laid a tiny egg on the caterpillar's back. Then she scrambled out of the nest and sealed it up again.

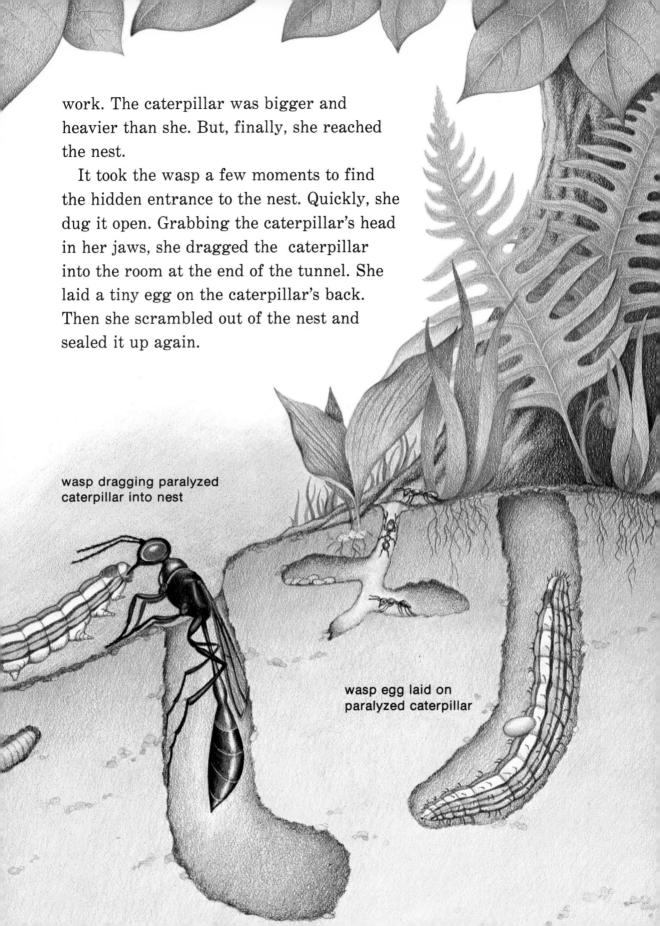

wasp dragging paralyzed
caterpillar into nest

wasp egg laid on
paralyzed caterpillar

She then flew away. During the next few days she would dig more nests and hunt more caterpillars to put in them.

A few days later, a tiny, wormlike baby wasp hatched in the dark nest. It had plenty of food—a whole caterpillar hundreds of times bigger than it.

Day after day, the baby ate and grew. In time, it had eaten the whole caterpillar. Then it spun a silk cocoon around itself.

By now, fall had come. All through fall and winter, the young wasp stayed wrapped in its cocoon. By the time spring came, the wasp was an adult. It broke out of the cocoon, dug its way out of the nest, and flew off. Now it ate only nectar from flowers. But if it were a female, it would someday hunt meat for its babies.

There are many different kinds of hunting wasps. Each kind hunts a different kind of prey. Some hunt beetles, some hunt flies, some hunt bees, some catch grasshoppers, some catch different kinds of caterpillars. One kind even hunts big tarantula spiders.

A nest of paper

An old log lay among a pile of dead leaves in a woods. A small winged creature came gliding through the air toward it—a young female hornet. She hovered a moment, then alighted beside the log. She crept beneath it and settled herself among the leaves.

It was late autumn, and the weather soon turned cold. Winter arrived, with its snowstorms and freezing days. The weather was often bitterly cold. The hornet lay motionless as the winter months passed.

In time, the air grew warmer. Spring sunshine filled the woods. One day, the hornet began to move. She wiggled her antennae. She twitched her wings. After a while, she flew up and circled about, looking around the woods. Last autumn she had mated. Now she wanted a good place to make a nest and start laying her eggs.

Settling on a tree, she scraped off a tiny bit of bark with her jaws. She chewed it into a wet paste. Then she flew up to a branch. She stuck the bit of paste onto the underside of the branch.

Back and forth she went, from the trunk of the tree to the branch, again and again. Each time, she added a bit of wood paste. She built a little cup, hanging down from a stem fastened to the branch. The paste quickly dried into a stiff, tough, grayish

paper. The hornet made several more paper cups, all joined together. Then she put a paper covering around them, with a hole in the bottom for an entrance.

In each of the cups, the hornet laid an egg. The eggs were sticky and stuck to the bottom of the cups.

Days passed, and the eggs began to hatch. Little, wormlike babies came out of the eggs. Each baby hung head downward, attached to its cup by a sort of glue that oozed out of the back of its body.

hornet's nest

This nest was opened up to show the inside. The yellowish shapes in many of the cells are larvae. Some cells have silk covers spun by older larvae. About ten days later, they tear off the covers and come out as adults. In a cell in the middle, there is an egg laid by the queen hornet.

The babies had to be fed, and their food was fresh meat. The mother hornet went hunting and killed a caterpillar. She chewed up bits of it and brought these to the babies. For a while, she spent most of her time bringing food to the babies.

The babies began to grow longer and fatter. Soon, they were so fat they didn't need glue to hold them in their cups—they fit so tightly that they couldn't fall out!

The mother hornet worked hard caring for her young. But, after a time, some of the

hornet

This hornet worker is adding paper to the outside of the nest. She chews wood into a ball of paste. Then she spreads the paste on the nest.

fat babies spun silk covers over their cups. Inside the covered cups, they began to change into adults. Before long, there were a number of grown-up daughters to begin helping their mother.

The daughters hunted insects and nectar, fed the babies, and worked on the nest. They added more groups of cups, covering them with walls of paper. The nest soon became a large oval ball.

All summer long, the nest bustled with activity. Thousands of hornets made it their home. Most were female workers. By the middle of summer, though, some males and some "princesses," who would some day be queens, had hatched.

But by the end of summer, the nest was dying. The males and the princesses flew away to mate. They did not come back. The old queen died. No more eggs were laid. Then the workers, too, began to die. By late autumn, the nest was silent and empty.

The insects we call hornets are really a kind of wasp. Many kinds of wasps and hornets live in hanging nests made of paper. But the hornets known as yellow jackets usually make their nests underground.

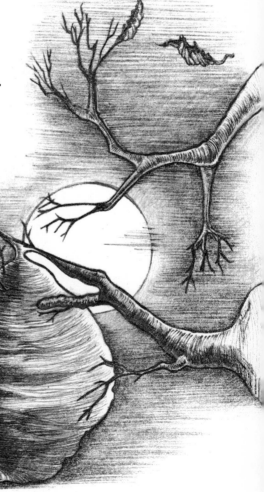

Bugs, Hoppers, and Fleas

cicada

Oh, stinkbug, stinkbug,
   Stop and think, bug;
You really must change your name!
   Although your aroma
Puts enemies in a coma,
   That's not the best way to gain fame!

Just look at the skunk
   And you'll think, as he's thunk,
That smelling bad's really no fun.
   Is there no other way
(Although *what*, I can't say)
   To send enemies off on a run?

For, a bad-smelling feller,
   Is an offense to the smeller,
That most people greatly deplore.
   Just get rid of your stink
And then people won't think
   To call you "stink" bug any more.

           A Suggestion to the Stinkbug
           Tom McGowen

Insect skunks

Stinkbugs are the skunks of the insect world. When a stinkbug is in danger, it sprays a bad-smelling and bad-tasting liquid out of openings near its back legs. This keeps a bird or other animal from eating it.

There are many kinds of stinkbugs. Most kinds have bodies shaped like the shields used by knights of old. In Great Britain, stinkbugs are usually called shieldbugs. Many kinds of stinkbugs are brightly colored, but some look like bits of bark. Some are the color of leaves.

A great many kinds of stinkbugs are harmful pests that spoil vegetables and fruit. But some stinkbugs are helpful. They eat harmful caterpillars and other insects.

Stinkbugs are members of the group of insects scientists call bugs. We often call any insect or tiny creature a bug. But true bugs are a particular group of insects. All true bugs have a sharp beak for a mouth.

Some bugs are tiny, and some are large. Some have wings; some do not. Most bugs live on land, but some live in water. Some true bugs, such as stinkbugs and water bugs, have "bug" as part of their name. But other "bugs," such as June bugs and potato bugs, belong to the beetle group. They are not true bugs.

back swimmer

Swimming bugs

A pond is a lively—and dangerous—place. It's full of small creatures that spend most of their time looking for some other creature to eat—or trying to keep from being eaten themselves! Three little creatures often found in ponds are true bugs. Because they live in water, they are called water bugs.

The back swimmer is a water bug that spends most of its time upside-down! Its body is shaped much like a boat—the underside is flat and the back is rounded, like the bottom of a boat. So, the back swimmer moves about on its back. It rows itself along, using its two hind legs like oars.

giant water bug

water boatman

The back swimmer is a hunter. It often lies in wait, holding onto a water plant, until it sees a mosquito larva, a baby fish, or a tadpole swimming above. Then it lets go of the plant, drifts upward, and seizes the creature from beneath. It jabs its long, sharp beak into its prey, and sucks out all the liquid. A back swimmer usually isn't much more than half an inch (1.3 centimeters) long. But it can give even a person a painful jab with its sharp beak.

The water boatman is another kind of water bug. It looks much like the back swimmer, but it swims right side up. Water boatmen stay near the bottom of a pond. They have short front legs that are covered with bristles. A water boatman uses these legs to sweep tiny plants and animals out of the mud and into its mouth.

The biggest of the water bugs are large insects, often more than two inches (5 cm) long. They are called giant water bugs. They are fierce hunters, and will chase after fish, frogs, and other creatures much bigger than themselves. Some are known as toe biters, because they nip at people who swim in their pond!

All the water bugs breathe air. They must come to the surface for fresh air. Though they live in water, water bugs do spend some time flying. On summer nights, they often fly around electric lights.

water strider

This water strider's feet make little dents as it walks on top of the water. The small insect is a stonefly the water strider killed for food.

Water walkers

The bug known as a water strider, or pondskater, can stand, run, and even jump, on top of the water of a quiet pond or pool. For the water strider, the surface of the water is like a thin, rubbery "skin," over the rest of the water. The water strider's feet will make little dents in the "skin," but they won't break through it.

When a water strider runs, it looks as if it is skating. It uses only four legs for running—the two middle ones and the two back ones. It uses its front legs like arms, to grab smaller insects. When it catches another insect, it jabs its sharp beak into the creature's body and sucks it dry.

Some kinds of water striders live on rivers. One kind even lives on the ocean. But, none of these creatures can swim. And if a water strider gets even one drop of water on its body, it will drown.

Assassins!

His big, bulging black eyes fixed upon his victim, the assassin attacks! The victim is much bigger, but it doesn't matter. The assassin stabs with his sharp, curved weapon. Poison flows into the victim's body!

The word *assassin* means "someone who kills with a sudden attack." That's a good description of the insects known as assassin bugs! Some hunt, others wait in ambush. When they find their prey, they make a sudden attack.

An assassin bug's "weapon" is a long, jointed tube with a sharp point. This tube curves down from the bug's mouth. The

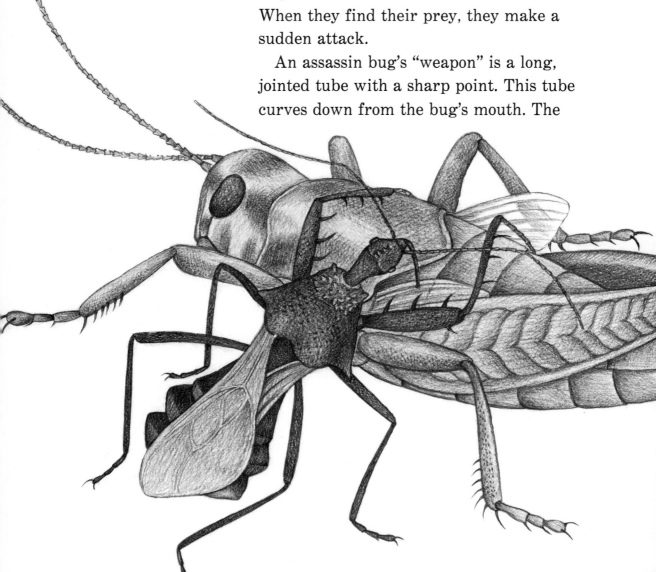

assassin bug holds its prey with its front legs and stabs the curved tube into the helpless creature. Poison shoots through the tube and paralyzes the victim. The assassin bug then sucks out all the blood and soft parts, leaving only a dry, empty shell.

There are many kinds of assassin bugs. In the United States and Canada, the spined assassin bug is common. In Great Britain, the heath assassin bug hunts insects and spiders. And in Australia, there's an assassin bug known as the "bee killer."

Some kinds of assassin bugs are helpful. They attack caterpillars that harm trees and insects that harm food plants. However, some of these bugs can give a person a very painful "bite" if they're touched!

Other kinds of assassin bugs are actually dangerous. They will bite sleeping people and suck their blood. Some of these assassin bugs carry a deadly disease.

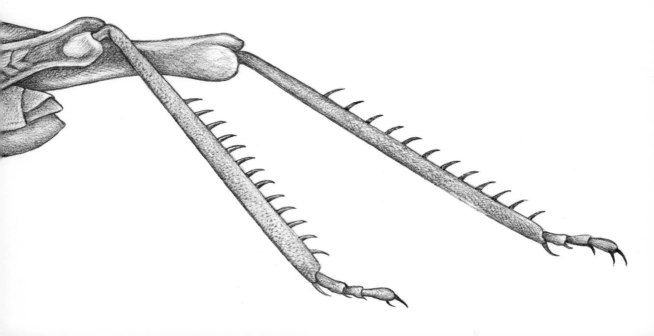

treehopper

Many kinds of treehoppers look just like a thorn when they sit on a twig. Because of this, these insects are known as thorn bugs.

Hoppers

Have you ever seen a thorn on a twig suddenly come to life and hop away? If so, it was really an insect—the kind called a hopper. Hoppers are hard to see, even when you're looking right at one. They're small, and often look like part of the plant they're sitting on.

There are many kinds of hoppers. The ones known as treehoppers are also called

thorn bugs. The hard skin on a thorn bug's back forms a high, curved point that looks just like a thorn. It is usually colored green or brown. When a thorn bug squats on a twig, it looks like a thorn.

Froghoppers sometimes look like tiny, big-eyed, green or brown tree frogs. They're also called spittlebugs. This is because the young have a strange way of protecting themselves.

Mother spittlebugs lay eggs on grass stems in the fall. In the spring, the young

spittlebug larva

After it hatches, a spittlebug larva covers itself with a foamy, sticky liquid that looks like spit. This protects it from sunlight and from enemies.

spittlebugs hatch. After a spittlebug hatches, it stands head downward on a blade of grass. It then squirts a mixture of air and sticky liquid out of its body. This bubbly, foamy stuff looks like spit—which is why this bug is called a spittlebug. The foamy stuff slides down over the spittlebug's body, covering it completely.

The spittlebug stays inside this foamy "tent" until it grows up. It eats by sipping juice out of the grass stem. The sticky foam protects it from most enemies and from the hot sun.

Leafhoppers usually have a green or greenish-yellow body. When they crouch on a leaf, they can hardly be noticed. But one kind of leafhopper is easy to see. Its red wings have greenish-blue stripes.

As you've probably guessed, hoppers got their name because they do a lot of hopping. They can make long, powerful leaps, from one plant to another. They can also fly.

It seems strange that such tiny creatures could cause people much trouble. But they do. They're very troublesome! They're all juice suckers that feed on many kinds of plants, and they do a great deal of damage. They cause the plants they feed on to wilt, to stop growing, and to catch diseases that kill them. Hoppers spoil potatoes, beets, celery, grapes, and many other plants people use for food.

treehopper
This South American treehopper looks like a dead leaf.

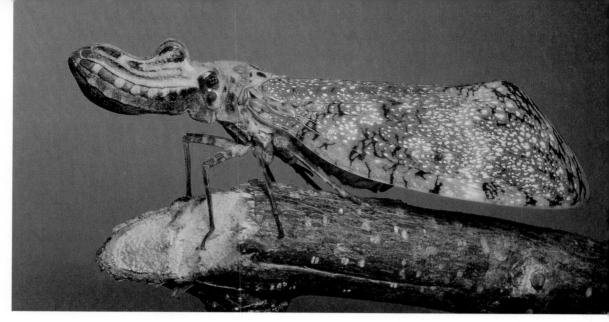

lantern fly

The front part of a lantern fly looks like an alligator's head. But this part is just a hollow "mask." The insect's real head is behind the fake one.

The alligator bug

The insect known as a lantern fly lives in South America. In spite of its name it doesn't glow like a lantern and it isn't a fly—it's a hopper. It's probably the strangest-looking of all insects. It seems to be trying to look like an alligator!

The front part of a lantern fly's head is a hollow shell shaped somewhat like a peanut. The way it is colored, it looks amazingly like the head of a toothy, big-eyed alligator. Because of this, the lantern fly is sometimes called an alligator bug.

It may be that this insect's alligator "mask" frightens some birds into leaving it alone. But, although the "mask" looks fierce, the lantern fly is harmless. Like all hoppers, it sucks plant juice. Its real head, eyes, and mouth parts are back behind the fake alligator head.

The red-eyed noisemakers

Every year, some part of the eastern half of the United States is invaded by red-eyed monsters!

The creatures appear in the springtime. On a night in May or June, they push up out of the ground by the tens of thousands. By morning, the ground is dotted with holes.

These creatures are little brown insects with big red eyes. Many people call them "seventeen-year locusts." But they aren't really locusts. Locusts are grasshoppers. These are cicadas (suh KAY duhz). Cicadas are relatives of the leafhoppers. Because they appear regularly after a certain period of years, scientists call them "periodical cicadas." However, there are so many groups of young cicadas, one or more groups appear somewhere every year.

The instant a cicada leaves the ground, it heads straight for the nearest tree. Soon, all the nearby trees are filled with the little creatures. If there are no trees, the cicadas will climb onto bushes, weeds, or even blades of grass. When the cicadas come out of the ground, they're not quite grown-up. They go into the trees and stay there until they are adults.

Each cicada clings to its perch and begins

to hump its back. The skin splits down the back, and the young cicada struggles out. It is yellowish-white, with two black spots on its back behind its red eyes. Slowly, two ragged bumps on its back swell up and become soft, white wings.

After a time, the cicada's body turns gray, then black. The wings become clear, shiny, and yellow, with orange veins in them. The cicada is now an adult and ready for life. For a female, this means mating and laying eggs. For a male, it mostly means making noise!

A few days after they become adults, the male cicadas begin to "sing" to attract females. The males sing all day long, and all

the cicada cycle—part 1

Cicada nymphs hatch from eggs that are laid in trees. The nymphs drop to the ground and crawl into small cracks in the earth. They will spend a number of years underground, sucking juice from tree roots and growing bigger.

together, by the thousands! The sound is a steady *bur-r-r* that people find very annoying. Fortunately, the cicadas don't sing at night—or it might be impossible for people to sleep!

A male periodical cicada makes noise the same way a drum does. And part of the cicada's body is like a drum. At the middle of the cicada's body, on each side, is an oval patch of thin skin. The cicada's body is hollow between the patches. The patches of stretched skin and the hollow body form a drum. The cicada "beats" the drum by making the skin patches vibrate.

A few days after a female mates, she begins laying eggs. At the end of her body

the cicada cycle—part 2
The cicada nymphs tunnel up out of the ground. They head for trees or bushes. Each nymph sheds its skin and becomes a winged adult. In time, the adults mate. The females lay eggs in branches and the cycle starts again.

adult cicada and old skin

Soon after a cicada nymph comes out of the ground, its skin splits open. The cicada crawls out of the old skin (bottom) as a winged adult.

she has a long, sharp tube. She uses this tube to bore rows of little slits in twigs. In each slit she lays about twenty-eight white, oblong eggs. Unfortunately, when there are a lot of female cicadas laying eggs, they often do great damage, especially to young trees.

For several weeks, the singing, the mating, and the egg-laying go on. Then, the cicadas begin to die. Soon, the ground beneath the trees is strewn with their bodies. The noise of the males' drums is heard no more.

After a few more weeks, the eggs in the twigs begin to hatch. The tiny nymphs have feelers and six legs. But when they hatch, they are wrapped in tight-fitting bags of skin they must first wiggle out of. Each nymph scurries along the twig, then drops off or is blown off, and drifts to the ground. Quickly, it goes underground, through the first crack in the earth it finds.

The nymph pushes down until it is about two feet (60 centimeters) underground. It finds a tree root into which it pushes its beak. Depending upon what kind of cicada it is, it will spend from three to seventeen years there, sucking juice from the root and growing. Then, one spring evening it will dig its way up out of the ground. And soon, there is a brand-new horde of red-eyed noisemakers.

Insect vampires

Fleas are insect vampires. They live on dogs, cats, birds, and other animals—and sometimes on people—and suck their blood!

A flea is a strange-looking creature. It has a very small head and no wings. Its sides are flat, so that it is like a coin standing on edge. This enables the flea to move easily between the hair or feathers on an animal's body. For the flea, this must be like walking through a forest of small trees, growing close together.

You might think that when a dog or cat scratches itself, its paw would easily push the fleas out of its fur. But all over a flea's back and underside are rows of long, stiff, flat spikes. These are like the teeth of a comb, pointing backwards. When a flea is pushed backward, its spikes catch on hair or feathers. It is wedged tight and can't be pushed loose. When the animal stops scratching, the flea just starts walking forward again.

You might also think that a dog or cat's hard claws would squash a flea. But a flea's skin is hard and tough. It's not easy to squash a flea. So, it's difficult for an animal to get rid of fleas!

Actually, a flea doesn't usually stay on the same animal very long. It moves from one animal to another, usually by jumping.

Fleas are amazing jumpers. They can leap as much as twelve to fifteen inches (30 to 37.5 centimeters). To match such a jump, a person would have to cover more than a quarter of a mile (about 396 meters) in a single leap!

Most kinds of fleas live on rats, mice, and other animals that live together in nests. A female flea lays eggs on an animal. When the eggs hatch, the young fleas drop off into the nest. They look like white worms, but they are so tiny you can't see them. They eat bits of dead plant and animal food they find in the nest. After a time, they make cocoons and become adults. When they come out of the cocoons, they hop onto the nearest animal.

Fleas are tiny insects, but they can be very dangerous. Fleas that live on rats can carry germs that cause terrible diseases. A little more than six hundred years ago,

dog fleas

A flea has a thin, flat body. This is why it is easy for fleas to walk between the hairs on a dog or other animal.

nearly twenty-five million people in Europe
died from a disease carried by rat fleas.
This disease was known as the Black Death.

The fleas had been sucking the rats' blood,
which was full of germs. When the fleas bit
people, they passed on the germs. The Black
Death, which is now called bubonic plague
(boo BAHN ihk playg), has struck in many
parts of the world. It has killed hundreds of
millions of people.

Today, there are ways of keeping bubonic
plague from spreading. Most places have
programs to get rid of rats and fleas. And
where people keep themselves clean and
healthy, fleas are not much of a problem.

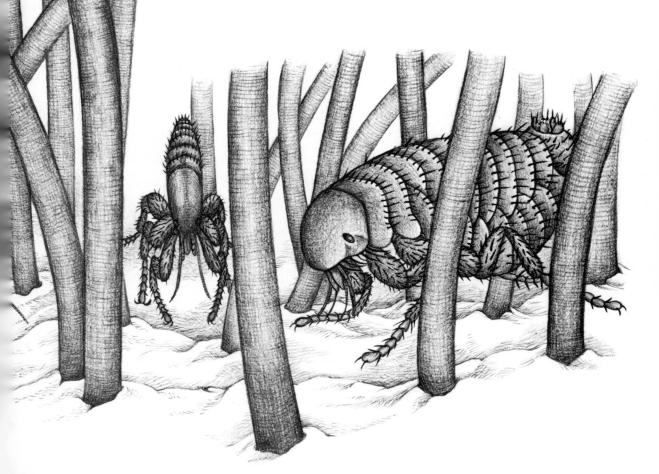

Hideaway insects

It is springtime in California. Tiny, tiny creatures are running about on the branches of a fruit tree. They are baby insects with six legs, feelers, and orange-yellow bodies. Their mouths are long sucking tubes, with a sharp point at the end.

One by one, the insects stop moving. As each one stops, it jabs its long tube down into the tree bark. It tucks its legs and feelers under its body. Soon, white, waxy threads start to ooze out of its body. Within two days, the insect is completely covered by a wax shell.

Twelve days later, the baby insect sheds its skin for the first time. The skin becomes part of the wax shell, making it harder. But, while most insects simply get bigger when they shed their skins, this insect changes tremendously. Its new body is very different. It no longer has eyes, feelers, or legs. It is just a round blob!

This creature is known as a scale insect. Its shell looks like a tiny scale on the tree branch. It is the kind of scale insect called a San Jose scale. This one is a female. She will never come out from under her scale. Hidden away, she will spend her life sucking juices out of the tree.

Male San Jose scales are very different.

oyster-shell scales

The scales on this tree look like oyster shells. Under each scale lives an insect. The insect makes its scale with a liquid from its body.

They have two wings, eyes, legs, and feelers—but no mouth. They don't need one. They leave their shells to find females and mate. Then they die.

The females give birth to live babies that come right out of their bodies instead of hatching from eggs. The babies are born under their mother's scale. They soon creep out to start their own scales. A female has about four hundred babies during a summer. The branches of a tree are soon covered with scales. In time, this can kill the tree.

There are many kinds of scale insects. They do not all look or live exactly as do the San Jose scales. But they all live on plants and suck the plant juices. Some scales look like tiny oyster shells, some like lumps of cotton. You may have seen scale insects in your house, without knowing it. The little reddish spots you sometimes see on an orange skin are scale insects!

Most scale insects are harmful. But, some are useful. One kind of scale insect, called lac scale, gathers by the hundreds of thousands in India and Burma. These insects give off a sticky stuff called lac. The name comes from a Persian word that means "hundred thousand." This sticky stuff is made into the clear, shiny varnish called shellac. It is used to protect and beautify wooden furniture.

Mosquitoes, Flies, and Lions

adult ant lion

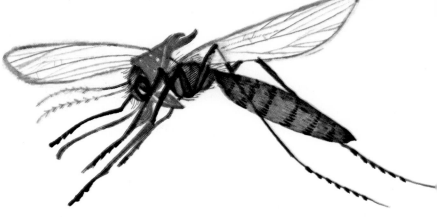

O Mrs. Mosquito quit biting me, please!
I'm happy my blood type with your type agrees.
  I'm glad that my flavor
  Has met with your favor
  I'm touched by your care;
  Yes, I'm touched everywhere:
On my arms and my legs, on my elbows and knees,
  Till I cannot tell which
  Is the itchiest itch
  Or which itch in the batch
  Needs the scratchiest scratch.
Your taste for my taste is the reason for these,
So Mrs. Mosquito, quit biting me, please!

                              Mosquito
                    Mary Ann Hoberman

The life of a mosquito

A cluster of slim, oblong objects floated on the surface of a small pond. There were nearly four hundred of them, jammed in a tight circle. But the circle was only about one-quarter of an inch (6 millimeters) across. The objects were the eggs of a single female mosquito (muh SKEE toh).

About a day after the female had laid the eggs, the first baby mosquito pushed its way through the bottom of its egg and into the water. It was a slim, wormlike creature. It had a large, round head with a dark eye on each side. There were two clumps of hairy bristles, like brushes, by its mouth.

With quick jerks of its body, the mosquito larva swam away from the circle of eggs. When it stopped swimming, the larva rose backward to the surface of the water. Poking a tube at the rear of its body up out of the water, the larva took in air, just as a skin diver breathes through a snorkel. Then it wriggled down to the bottom of the pond for its first meal.

The larva ate tiny plants and animals so small you would need a microscope to see them. Rapidly wiggling the brushes on its mouth, the larva made currents that pulled the creatures into its mouth.

The larva was in constant danger. Deadly dragonfly nymphs lay in ambush on rocks

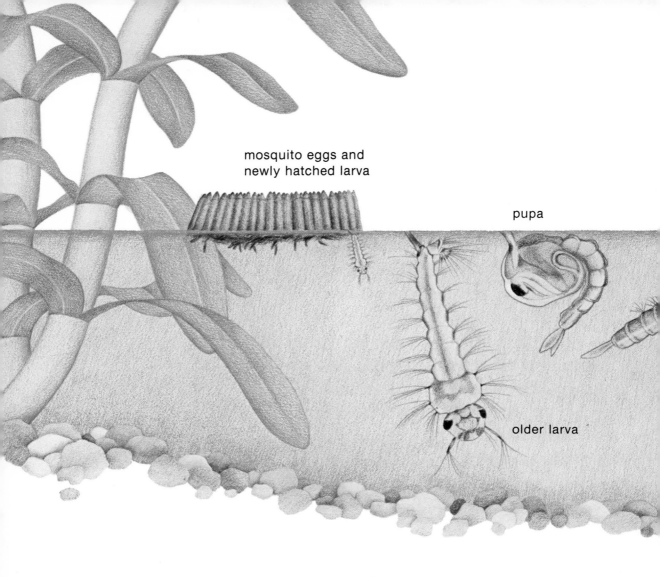

mosquito eggs and
newly hatched larva

pupa

older larva

and plants throughout the pond. Back
swimmers sped through the water in search
of prey. But the larva survived. For about a
week after it had hatched, it ate and grew.
It shed its skin three times. After the third
time, it changed into a pupa.

The pupa hung just under the surface of
the water, its body bent into the shape of a
comma. It stopped eating. But, unlike the
pupae of most insects, the mosquito pupa
could move. Once, frightened by a frog, it

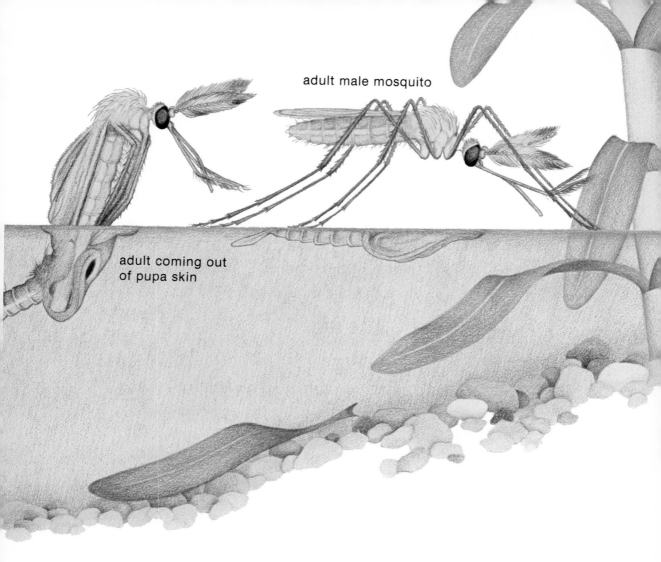

adult male mosquito

adult coming out
of pupa skin

swam quickly down to the bottom. Later, it
rose to the surface again.

After two days, the pupa's skin split. A
male mosquito climbed out. He was a slim,
long-legged creature with feathery feelers
and two wings. All insects with two wings
belong to the fly group. In fact, the name
mosquito is Spanish for "little fly."

After a time, the mosquito took to the air.
He skimmed toward the edge of the pool
and landed on a flower. The mosquito's

mouth was a long tube. He poked this tube into the flower and sucked up a meal of sweet nectar.

Other mosquitoes soon began to come out of the pond. At first, all were males. Then females appeared. As time passed, the humming of hundreds of mosquitoes filled the air. This humming came from the beating of the mosquitoes' wings, which beat about a thousand times a second.

The next evening, the male joined the other males in a "dance." They flew up in a great swarm. Then, all facing the same way, they rose and fell, rose and fell, in the air. Beneath them danced a swarm of females. From time to time, a female would rise up and fly straight among the males.

Once, the "ears" on the male's antennae told him a female was heading toward him. He could tell it was a female because the beating of her wings made a higher humming sound than that of a male. He moved to meet her. Together, they left the dancing swarm and glided downward to mate.

The male lived for only a week after mating. The female had a longer life. Gradually, she wandered farther from the pool. From time to time, she took nectar from a flower. But then she began to feel a need for a different kind of food.

She flew through the woods, searching.

Soon, something warm attracted her. The heat came from the body of a flying squirrel on a tree branch. The female mosquito settled on him.

Her mouth was different from that of the male mosquito. Male mosquitoes cannot "bite." But the females can. They have six needle-sharp points at the end of the sipping tube. The female jabbed her tube into the squirrel's skin and sucked up a small amount of blood. Then she flew on.

Much later, she came to a ditch filled with rain water. Skimming down, she laid several hundred eggs on the surface of the water. In days to come, she'd take more meals of blood and lay more eggs. After about a month, she would die.

Our worst enemy

What is the most dangerous animal in the world to people? A shark? A tiger? A poisonous snake? It's none of these. It's actually the common housefly! Why? Because flies carry germs.

Female houseflies lay about a hundred eggs at a time, usually on garbage or rotting food. The babies start feeding on the garbage as soon as they hatch. They are tiny, white wormlike things without legs. They are called maggots.

After five or six days, a maggot's skin becomes a thick, brown shell. Inside the shell, the maggot changes into an adult fly with two wings.

Because a fly tastes with its feet, it usually walks all over things "trying them out." In this way, it often gets germs on its feet. If it then walks on people's food, it leaves germs on the food.

Flies also spread germs when they eat. A fly can only suck up liquids. It can also turn some things into liquids. It does this by dissolving them with a liquid it "spits up" from its stomach.

A fly may suck up liquid that has germs in it. This puts the germs into the fly's stomach. If the fly then "spits up" some of its stomach liquid on the sugar at your table, the germs get on the sugar. If you eat

housefly

the sugar, the germs get into you. So, houseflies are dangerous and pesky.

But the flies that come into your house are not all houseflies. There are many kinds of the two-winged creatures called flies. Many are bothersome, but not all are dangerous. Some are even helpful—they carry pollen from one flower to another, helping new plants grow.

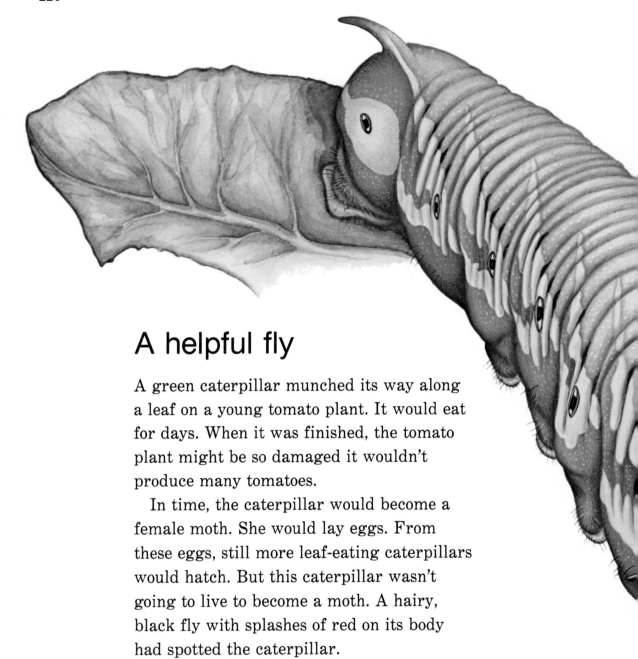

A helpful fly

A green caterpillar munched its way along a leaf on a young tomato plant. It would eat for days. When it was finished, the tomato plant might be so damaged it wouldn't produce many tomatoes.

In time, the caterpillar would become a female moth. She would lay eggs. From these eggs, still more leaf-eating caterpillars would hatch. But this caterpillar wasn't going to live to become a moth. A hairy, black fly with splashes of red on its body had spotted the caterpillar.

The fly landed beside the caterpillar, near its head. A long tube pushed out from the back end of the fly's body. Out of the tube came a number of small, white eggs. They were sticky, and stuck to the caterpillar's side.

The fly buzzed off, her work done. In a short time, little wormlike maggots would tear their way out of the eggs. Then they would bore into the caterpillar's body. Once inside, they would eat and eat, until nothing much was left of the caterpillar but its skin!

The flies known as tachina (TAK uh nuh) flies are very helpful to people. Female tachina flies lay their eggs on the larvae of many insects that spoil cabbages, corn, fruit, and other foods. The tachina fly maggots eat the larvae that would otherwise grow up and lay millions of eggs. These flies are among the best insect helpers we have!

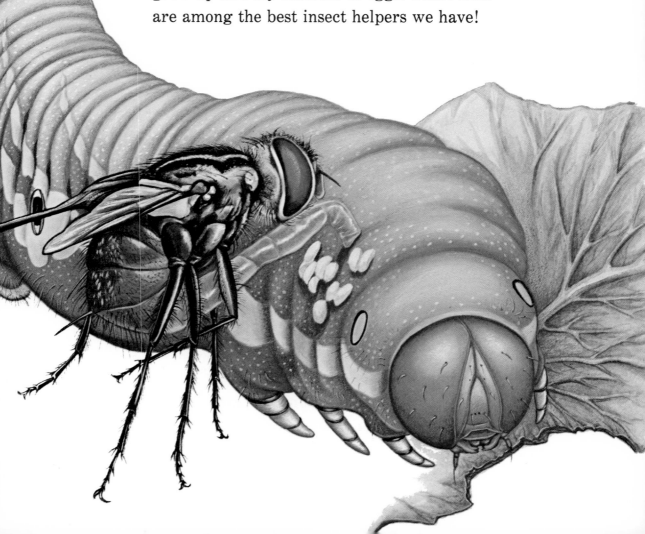

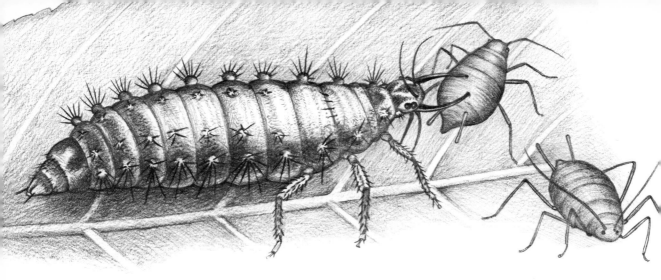

Lacewings

Green lacewings are quite pretty creatures. They have slim bodies, lacy wings, and big, golden eyes. They are also fierce hunters. They eat aphids and other insects that damage plants.

Lacewings lay their eggs on the tips of long, threadlike stems attached to the leaves of plants. When a baby lacewing hatches, it climbs down the stalk and goes hunting. It prowls over leaves in search of aphids, which it happily eats by the dozen!

A lacewing larva has long, curved jaws that come to a point. There is a deep groove in each jaw. The larva stabs its jaws deep into an aphid and lifts it into the air. The aphid's blood runs down the grooves and into the larva's mouth.

The larva has bunches of hairs sticking up like spikes all over its back. After it drains an aphid dry, it often sticks the crumpled, empty skin onto the hairs. It may also stick bits of bark, moss, and other

adult green lacewing
If a lacewing is touched, it will give off a bad smell. For this reason, lacewings are also known as "stink flies."

things onto itself. It soon looks like a walking garbage heap!

After a lacewing larva has shed its skin several times, it spins a silk cocoon around itself. In about two weeks, it comes out an adult. But it doesn't break its way out, as many insects do. It makes a neat, round door with a "hinge"!

An adult lacewing is just as ferocious an aphid hunter as it was when it was a larva. Many people call lacewings stink flies. This is because they give off a very bad smell if they're touched.

Underwater builders

Caddis flies, or sedge flies, are small,
winged insects that look like moths. Adult
caddis flies don't do anything unusual—but
young caddis flies certainly do. With sand,
sticks, stones, and leaves, they build houses
that look like horns, domes, log cabins, and
snail shells!

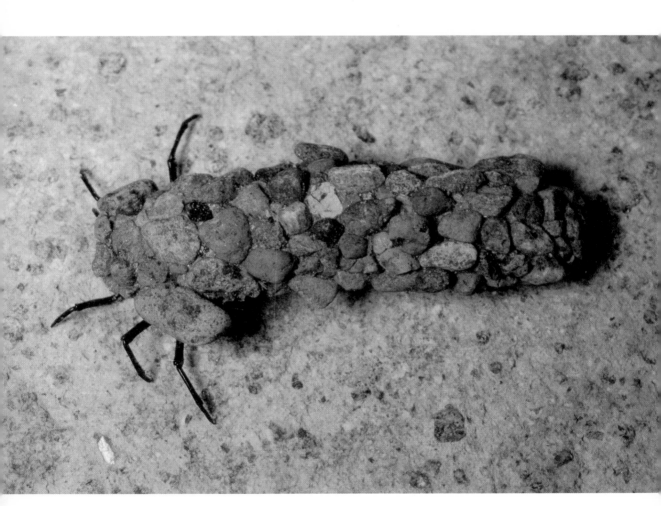

a caddis fly larva in its artificial shell

Caddis fly larvae hatch from eggs that the females lay on rocks, logs, or plants in ponds, rivers, and streams. A caddis fly larva looks like a caterpillar with six long legs. As soon as it hatches, it begins to build its house.

There are many different kinds of caddis flies. Each kind makes a different sort of house. One kind of house is a "mobile home" that the larva drags around with it! This is really a sort of artificial shell that the larva builds around itself.

One kind of shell, made of sand, looks like a long, pointed horn. Another kind is a bumpy dome made of pebbles. Still another is a "log cabin," made of crisscrossed sticks. The larva fastens the materials together with silk it spins, and with a glue that comes out of its body.

Other kinds of caddis fly larvae build houses out of sand, pebbles, and silk. Near their houses, they weave silken nets or funnels to catch small insects, tiny crabs, and baby fish.

When a caddis fly larva is ready to become an adult, it pulls all the way into its shell or house. Inside its skin, its body changes. After a time, it swims to the top of the water. Its skin splits and out crawls a winged adult. Although adult caddis flies have wings, they also swim and even run on top of the water.

adult caddis fly

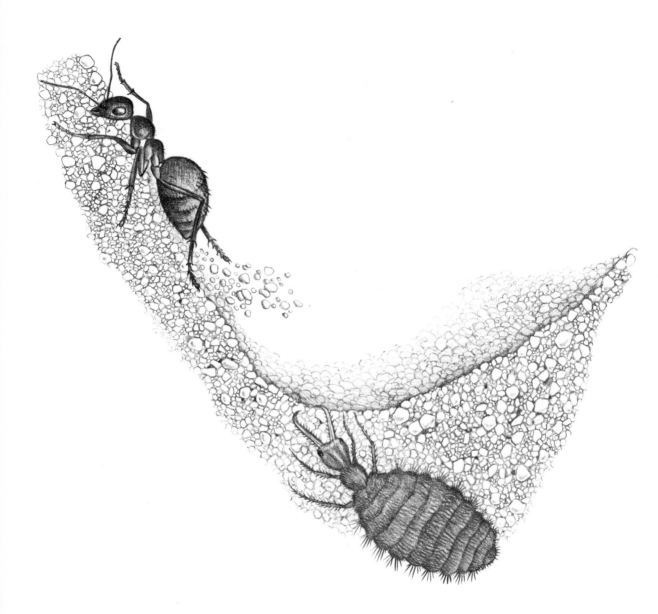

A trap maker

An ant scurried about on a sandy patch of ground. Suddenly, the soft sand slid out from under its feet. It was sliding down the steep side of a pit. It scrambled to try and stop. Then a shower of sand spattered the

ant. It lost its balance completely and tumbled to the bottom of the pit.

At once, it was seized by powerful, curved jaws. The ant had fallen into a trap made by an ant lion!

An ant lion has a plump, hairy body, one-quarter inch to an inch (about 6-25 millimeters) long. Often called a doodlebug, it is the larva of a winged insect that looks like a dragonfly.

Soon after an ant lion hatches, it digs a small pit with steep, slanting sides. It starts by walking backward in a circle. (The ant lion can walk only backward.) It pushes its tail into the sand, like a shovel. The sand slides over the ant lion's flat back, toward its head. When the ant lion jerks its head, it throws up a shower of sand.

The ant lion lies at the bottom of the pit, with its head sticking out of the sand. When an ant or other insect starts to slide into the pit, the ant lion throws sand at it so that the creature will keep sliding. Then the ant lion seizes its prey in its jaws and squirts poison into it. After it sucks the creature dry, the ant lion flips it out of the pit.

In cold weather, an ant lion burrows down under the sand to wait for spring. When an ant lion is ready to become an adult, it forms its cocoon under the sand. It comes out of the cocoon as a long, slim, flying creature with lacy wings.

Silverfish and Springtails

silverfish

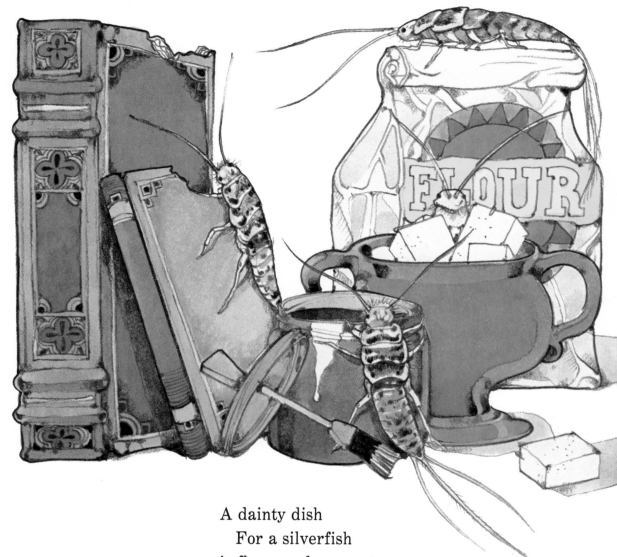

A dainty dish
　　For a silverfish
is flour, and sugar, too.
　　But they've also a taste
For old dried paste,
　　And laundry starch, and glue!
(A secret I'll share—
　　I sure wouldn't care
To eat such stuff—would you?)

　　　　　　　　An Odd Appetite
　　　　　　　　Tom McGowen

Silverfish

The insects known as silverfish are pests that live in people's houses. They don't like light, so in daytime they hide in cracks and dark places. They come out at night to eat.

Because of their odd appetite, silverfish cause damage. They eat the paste off wallpaper, so that the paper comes loose. They eat the glue in bookbindings, making books fall apart. And they eat starch in clothes, making holes in the cloth. They're also fond of flour and sugar.

Silverfish are different from most insects in many ways. For one thing, most insects have wings. Even ants are winged insects that have lost their wings—except, of course, for the queens and males. And many insects that almost never fly, such as cockroaches, have wings. They just don't use them. However, silverfish are truly wingless insects.

Most young insects don't look at all like their parents. But a baby silverfish looks just like an adult, only much smaller. Like humans, baby silverfish simply grow bigger and finally become adults.

Like all growing insects, young silverfish must shed their skin from time to time. But, unlike other insects, a silverfish keeps on shedding its skin even after it has become an adult.

Springtails

A fat-bodied insect crawled slowly among the dead, wet leaves on the forest floor. Suddenly, a spiderlike creature appeared. It darted at the insect.

Spang! The insect vanished just before the creature could grab it! The insect hadn't flown away, because it had no wings. And it hadn't jumped. It had used its own special defense.

The insect was a springtail. It was given this name because of a fork-shaped "spring" at the rear of its body.

Most of the time, a springtail holds its "spring" tight against the underside of its body. But when a springtail snaps its "spring" out, it whips against the ground. The springtail shoots three or four inches (7.5 to 10 centimeters) into the air. It lands about a foot (30 cm) away. This is how it escapes from spiderlike mites, centipedes, and other enemies.

Springtails are hard to see because they are very tiny. They usually hide in the ground or among piles of leaves. Sometimes they look like black specks on a plant.

You've probably never seen a springtail. Yet there are more springtails around you than almost any other kind of insect. If you dug up a spoonful of soil almost anywhere in the world, there probably would be at least two springtails in it!

Springtails live in meadows, forests, gardens, sandy beaches, ponds and pools, and in flowerpots. Some even live in the ice and snow of the Arctic and Antarctic, where no other insects can survive.

Springtails are both harmful and helpful. Some kinds eat plants and cause damage on farms and in gardens. Some eat mushrooms and are pests to mushroom growers. But many kinds of springtails help keep the soil moist and fertile. And some help keep the world clean because they eat dead plants and animals.

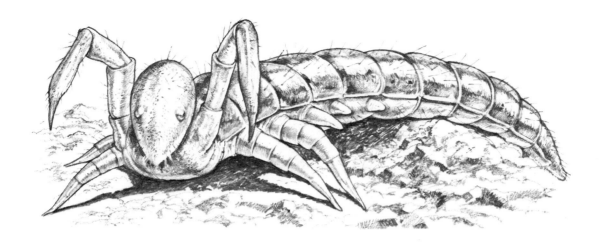

Pretend antennae

In moist soil, under piles of moldy leaves, and in decaying logs live strange, tiny insects called proturans (proh TYUR uhnz). They're not much bigger than the point of a pin. Proturans are different from all other insects. They are the only insects that don't have antennae, or feelers. And they don't have eyes.

If you had to walk through a pitch-black place, you'd probably stretch out your arms to feel your way along. And that's just what proturans do. As a proturan walks about, it holds out its two front legs and feels its way around.

A proturan has a long, wormlike body and no wings. It looks more like a worm with legs than an insect. When it holds out its front legs, it almost looks like a worm pretending to be an insect with antennae!

Web spinners

You might think that a creature known as a web spinner would be some kind of spider. But web spinners are actually odd little insects that spin silk.

The silk made by most insects comes out of their mouth. And a spider's silk comes out of its back. But a web spinner's silk comes out of its two front feet.

Web spinners eat dead leaves, grass, moss, bark, and the plants called lichens (LY kuhnz). They build their communities where there's a good food supply. This might be under a pile of dead leaves, under loose bark on tree roots, or among lichens.

A web spinner community is made up of many connecting tunnels. And all of the tunnels are made of silk! From twenty to several hundred web spinners may live in a community.

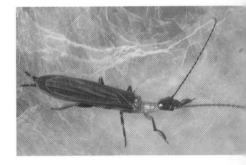

male web spinner

Female web spinners lay their eggs in the tunnels. They watch over the eggs carefully. When the tiny nymphs hatch, their mothers take good care of them. The nymphs never leave the tunnels until they're grown up. Even the littlest nymphs can make silk and often help spin new tunnels.

Some kinds of male web spinners have wings and sometimes fly. But some males don't have wings. And the females never have wings.

Earwigs

How did the insect called an earwig get its odd name? No one is sure. But at one time, this insect was known as an *earwicga*, or "ear beetle." People gave it this name because they believed it would crawl into their ears! Earwigs don't do this, however.

mother earwig and eggs

Mother earwigs take good care of their eggs and of the babies that hatch from them.

The name may also have come from the shape of the earwig's back wings. These wings are shaped somewhat like a human ear. The name may simply have been shortened from earwing to earwig.

It's easy to recognize an earwig. It has a long body with big, pointed pincers, like a pair of pliers, at the back end. However, you won't often see earwigs. They hide during the day and come out at night.

Earwigs eat almost anything—fruit, vegetables, flower petals, dead plants and animals, insect eggs, caterpillars, and snails. Although most kinds of earwigs have wings, they seldom fly. They spend most of their time running about on the ground.

An earwig uses its tail pincers mostly to defend itself. If it is in danger, it raises its tail and spreads the pincers. It can squeeze ants that try to attack it, and it can even give a human a painful pinch. Some earwigs use their pincers to catch caterpillars and other creatures.

Most insect mothers lay their eggs and then go away. They never see the babies that hatch. But not earwigs. They lay their eggs in little "rooms" they dig in the earth. They watch over the eggs and lick them to keep them clean. When the nymphs hatch, the mother keeps an eye on them. She makes sure they don't stray until they're big enough to look after themselves!

Spiders and Such

spider

The spider weaves his silver wire
Between the cherry and the briar.

He runs along and sees each thread
Well-fastened on each hawser-head.

And then within his wheel he dozes
Hung on a thorny stem of roses,

While fairies ride the silver ferry
Between the rose-bud and the cherry.

Of a Spider
Wilfrid Thorley

How a spider spins a web

Say "spider" and most people think of a
web. Usually, they'll think of what is called
an orb web. It's the kind people notice
because it's pretty. The threads stretch out
from the center like the spokes of a wheel.
Other threads connect the spokes and form
many circles, one inside another.

Suppose you wanted to make a giant orb
web, just the way a spider does. You'd need
thousands of yards (meters) of rope and
gallons of glue. You'd also have to climb up
and down a rope and walk a tightrope!

To begin, you fasten one end of a length of
rope high up in a tree. Then you climb
down and carry the other end of the rope to
a tree about seventy or eighty feet (21 to 23
m) away. You climb this tree and fasten the
rope so that it stretches between the two
trees like a tightrope. (Of course, a spider's
tightrope would only stretch between two
little twigs. But this is as far for the spider
as the distance between the trees is for you!)

Now, walk a short way out along the
tightrope. There, you fasten another rope.
Let this rope hang down to the ground.
Slide down the hanging rope and fasten the
end in the ground.

Next, climb a short way back up the
hanging rope and attach a third rope.
Holding the end of the third rope, climb all

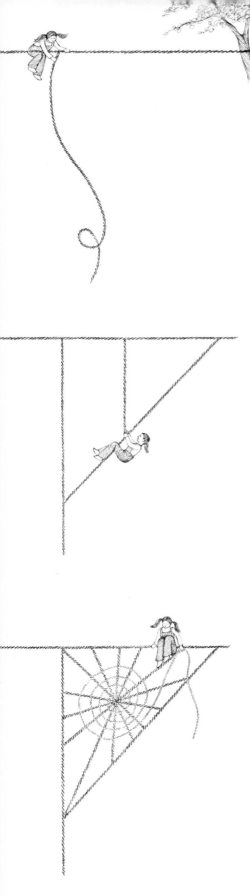

the way up to the tightrope. Run about fifty feet (15 m) along the tightrope and tie the end of the third rope to the tightrope. Now you have a triangle between the two trees.

But this is just the beginning. Next, you must hang a rope from the middle of the tightrope. Slide down this rope and fasten it to the third rope. Then climb about halfway back up. There, tie on about a dozen other ropes. You then have to climb around and tie these ropes to the triangle so that they are like the spokes of a wheel. Next, comes the long job of making all the circles that connect the spokes. Finally, you have to coat the circles with glue.

You can see now what an amazing thing a spider web is, and how hard a spider works to spin one. Some orb webs are two feet (60 centimeters) wide. If a spider were as big as a person, such a web would be about 144 feet (33 m) wide!

A spider spins its silk "rope" in its body. The silk squirts out of tubes, called spinnerets, that are at the back end of the spider's body. The silk comes out as a liquid, but dries and hardens as it hits the air. The spider can make either dry or sticky silk.

When its web is finished, the orb-weaver spider hangs underneath the middle of the

spider web

This female garden spider is sitting in the center of her orb web. The web is covered with dew.

web or hides nearby. An insect that flies, jumps, or crawls into the web is stuck fast at once. When the insect struggles to free itself, the web shakes. This lets the spider know that something is caught. The spider then hurries toward the trapped insect. An oily liquid on the spider's body and feet keep it from getting stuck in its own web.

The spider uses some of its eight legs to grab the trapped creature. It turns the insect over and over, spraying it with sheets of silk. The insect soon looks like a mummy. Then the spider carries the helpless insect back to the center of the web, to be eaten.

A captured insect usually damages the web with its struggles. Some orb weavers repair their web right away. Some make a whole new web after they've caught two or three insects. And others just let their web get ragged and tattered.

A grass spider's trap

A bee buzzed briskly along through the air. Zooming down, it steered its way between the branches of a leafy bush.

Suddenly, the bee found itself flying among a vast tangle of long, white "ropes." These tightly stretched "ropes" crisscrossed every which way in the bee's path. The bee crashed into several of them and tumbled straight down!

The bee fell only a short distance. It landed on a wide, flat sheet made of silken "ropes" woven together. Before the bee could gather its senses and fly off, an eight-legged shape rushed at it. Sharp fangs sank into the bee's body, squirting poison. The bee had been caught in the trap of a grass spider.

You will often see a grass spider's web on a lawn or in a bush. It looks much like a piece of gauzy cloth stretched over the grass or leaves. If you look closely, you'll see the glistening tangle of threads crisscrossing above it—a barrier for flying insects to bump into. And you'll also see that one edge of the flat sheet forms a tube, like a funnel. That's where the spider hides, only the tips of two of its legs peeping out.

Because of the funnel-shaped hiding place, this kind of web is called a funnel

funnel web

web. A funnel web isn't sticky like an orb web. But it is soft and spongy, so that an insect has a hard time moving on it. However, the spider can move across it very quickly.

Funnel webs are often large and thick. Long ago, people sometimes used them as bandages.

grass spider in a funnel web
The spider is just inside the entrance to the funnel part of the web. The part above the funnel spreads out to form a broad sheet. This part of the web is wet from rain.

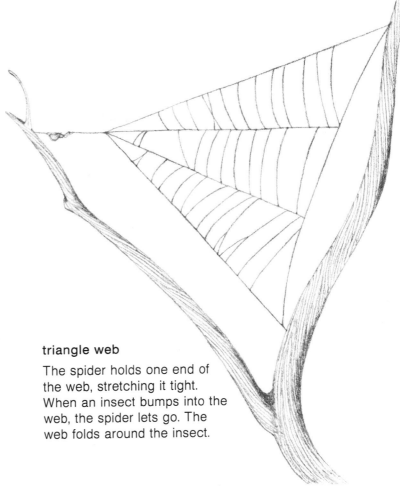

triangle web

The spider holds one end of the web, stretching it tight. When an insect bumps into the web, the spider lets go. The web folds around the insect.

A world of webs

Many kinds of spiders spin webs to catch flying insects. Each kind of spider makes its own special kind of web—from small, sticky traps to large, tightly woven nets. Here are pictures of three very different kinds of webs.

ladder web

This web is about three feet (91 centimeters) long. Flying moths that bump into it near the top slide to the bottom. There, the spider grabs them.

filmy-dome web

Flying insects that bump into the threads above the dome fall onto the dome. The spider, hanging under the dome, pulls them through.

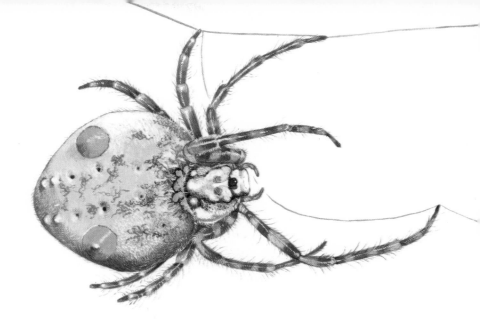

The bolas spider

The fat little spider crouched down, hugging a twig. All day, as the sun shone on the tree, she hardly moved. But as the sun finally set and shadows filled the woods, the spider came to life.

She scurried out onto the end of a branch. There, she attached a silken thread to the bark with a dab of sticky silk. Moving a short distance along the branch, she pasted down the other end of the thread. The thread now hung from the branch in a loop, like a swing.

The spider crept out onto the thread. She spun another piece of thread, about two inches (5 centimeters) long. Then she squirted some sticky silk on the end of the thread to form a gooey ball. Holding this line and ball with one of her mouthparts and one leg, she waited.

A great many moths and other night

insects began to appear. They swooped and
fluttered among the trees. After many
minutes, a moth skimmed by the spider.

At once, she swung her line out toward
the moth. The gob of glue on the end struck
the moth's body with a plop—and stuck.
Desperately, the moth tried to flutter
away. But the silk thread attached to the
ball of glue held it fast. Quickly, the
spider pulled the line toward her, until
she was able to grab the struggling moth
and give it a poisonous bite.

This little spider that catches insects
by throwing a sticky line at them is called
a bolas spider. A bola, or bolas, is a
length of rope with a steel ball at each
end. South American cowboys use it to catch
runaway steers or calfs. The weight of the
balls makes the rope wind around the
animal's legs, so that the animal can't
move. The bolas spider's line and ball of
glue work somewhat the same way.

Hunting with a net

The ogre-faced spider got its name because of its two huge, staring eyes. These two eyes are much bigger than the spider's other six eyes. They make this creature look like a scary ogre, or monster.

The ogre-faced spider hunts in somewhat the same way as a bolas spider. But the ogre-faced spider captures its prey with a net!

During the day, an ogre-faced spider stays pressed flat against the bark of a tree. Its thin, brown body looks like a bit of bark. At twilight, the spider moves onto a "platform" of tangled silk threads it has fastened to the tree trunk. Then it spins a net of crisscrossed threads of sticky silk.

The spider hangs by its back legs from its platform, or from a silk line. It holds its net in its front legs. When a moth flies near enough, the spider throws itself forward and flings the net over the prey. The net stretches to cover even quite large moths. Quickly, the spider bites the captured insect and wraps it in silk. Then the spider eats.

Trap-door spiders

Some kinds of spiders live in an
underground burrow, or tunnel, with a
door, or lid, that opens and closes. The door
even has hinges and a "handle" on the
inside!

These spiders are known as trap-door
spiders. A young trap-door spider digs a
tunnel in the earth. It lines the tunnel with
silk—like a room covered with thick
curtains. Then the spider makes a round
door out of layers of dirt and silk. This is
fastened to the entrance. The door is quite
thick and fits into the entrance like a cork
in a bottle.

The outside of the door is made to look
like the ground all around the tunnel. When
the door is closed, the entrance can hardly
be seen. If there is moss on the ground near
the entrance, the spider will plant some
moss on the door to help hide it.

A male trap-door spider only leaves his
nest once in his life, to move in with a
female and mate. A female never leaves her
nest. The nest is an ambush—a place from
which the spider can make a surprise attack
on its prey.

When a trap-door spider is hungry, it
lurks at the tunnel entrance. It holds the
door slightly open so that it can peep out.
Then it lies in wait until an insect comes by.

trapdoor spider

A trapdoor spider sits in the entrance to its burrow, waiting for prey to come near.

When an insect comes close enough, the spider reaches out and grabs it. The spider gives the insect a bite with its poisonous fangs, to paralyze it. Then it drags the insect into the nest and eats it.

Sometimes, a trap-door spider's nest becomes a fort. Wasps and other enemies may try to break in. The spider has to keep its door locked against them. On the inside of the door are two holes that form the "handle." The spider slips its fangs into these holes and pulls. It also braces its legs against the sides of the tunnel. When the spider uses all its strength to hold the door shut, even a person has difficulty getting it open.

Unfortunately, some of the spider's enemies, such as wasps, are able to chew through the door. Then the spider has to fight for its life.

Some kinds of trap-door spiders don't depend on a thick door to save them. Their front door is made mostly of silk and is quite thin. But these spiders have a trick they play if an enemy breaks through the door. They have a small side tunnel, branching off the main tunnel. This side tunnel has a door that can be pulled shut to close it off, or that can be pushed up to close off the main tunnel. The door blends in perfectly with the tunnel walls. An enemy is often tricked into thinking the tunnel is empty!

One kind of trap-door spider uses part of its body as an extra "door." The spider's back part is very large, hard, and flat across the end. If an enemy breaks down the spider's front door, the spider turns around and goes down its tunnel, headfirst. The tunnel is narrower near the bottom, and the spider's back part is soon wedged in tightly. It forms a thick, hard "door," that an enemy can't bite, sting, or chew through. Finally, the enemy just gives up and goes away!

Life in a silken tube

A female purse-web spider never sets foot outside her house. She gets her food by pulling it right through the wall!

A purse-web spider's house is partly underground and partly above ground. The

female purse-web spider

a female purse-web spider inside her tunnel

underground part is a deep tunnel at the foot of a tree. This tunnel is lined with silk. The part above ground is a long tube of silk. This tube stretches up the side of the tree. The tube was named a purse-web long ago, because it looked like the kind of purse ladies once carried.

The female purse-web spider spends most of her time inside the tunnel. But she can hear or feel when an insect crawls over her silken tube. She runs "upstairs," inside the tube. She bites right through the silk, sinking her poison fangs into the insect. When the insect can no longer move, the spider slits open the wall and drags the creature inside.

After the spider eats, she pushes what is left of her prey out the top of the tube. Later, she repairs the slit in the wall.

A male purse-web spider lives in much the same way as a female. But males do leave home after a time, to look for females. A male wanders about until he finds a tube that belongs to a female. He drums on it with his claws. This tells the female that he is a spider, like her, and not an insect to be attacked.

After a time—when he feels it's safe—the male slits open the tube and goes inside. He and the female mate. Then the male stays in the nest until he dies—or, until the female eats him!

Wolves, lynxes, and crabs

The hunter watched from his tower. From there, he could see better than from the ground. With keen eyes, he peered out, waiting to catch sight of some animal that might become his prey.

Ah! He saw an animal in the distance! At once, the hunter left his tower and sped over the ground. His prey didn't see him until it was too late. The hunter leaped. He seized the animal in his front legs and crushed it with his sharp, powerful jaws!

The hunter was the kind of spider that's known as a wolf spider. Wolf spiders got their name because they get their food just as a wolf does—by running after it. And, like wolves, these spiders are fast runners and have sharp eyes.

Many kinds of wolf spiders make burrows to hide in. The burrow may be a shallow pit under a stick or stone, or a deep tunnel in the ground. Some wolf spiders build a tower of dirt, grass, and twigs over their burrow. They use the tower as a lookout. They crouch there, peering eagerly for their prey.

Other wolf spiders lurk in their burrows, waiting for an insect to come into sight. Then they leap out and chase it. Still other kinds of wolf spiders prefer to prowl about instead of lying in ambush.

Mother wolf spiders take their babies

wolf spider and babies

After her eggs hatch, a mother wolf spider carries her babies on her back wherever she goes. After about a week, the babies leave her.

with them wherever they go—both before and after the eggs hatch. When a mother wolf spider lays eggs, she makes a round bag, or sac, of silk in which to keep them. The sac is nearly as big as she is. She fastens it to her spinnerets and drags it behind her.

The eggs hatch inside the sac. The mother seems to know when all the eggs have hatched. She bites open the sac and the babies come out. They climb onto her back until she is nearly covered with tiny spiderlings! The spiderlings ride on her back wherever she goes—even when she chases prey. After about a week, the babies have shed their skin and grown a little bigger. Then they leave their mother, to begin their own lives as swift hunters.

Another kind of spider does its hunting among the leaves of trees and bushes. These hunters are known as lynx spiders. They are named for the lynx, a catlike animal that is a quick, skillful hunter.

Lynx spiders scurry over leaves and leap from twig to twig. They are as quick and as keen-eyed as wolf spiders. Many are greenish in color, and blend into the leaves. Lynx spiders don't carry their egg sac around. They fasten it to a leaf or branch, or hang it in a little netlike web.

The spiders known as crab spiders are

lynx spider and egg sac

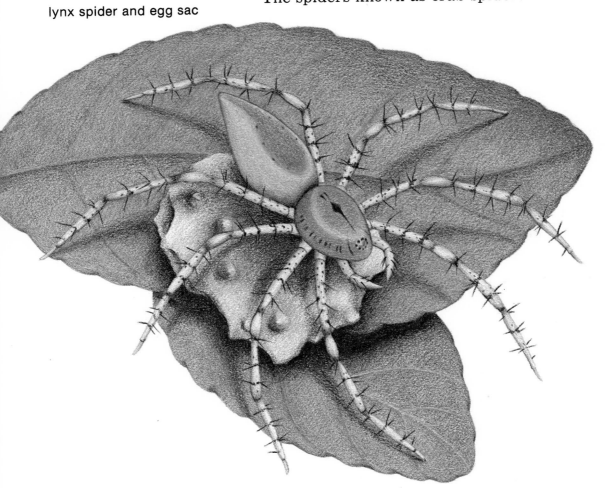

a honeybee falls
prey to a crab spider

Some crab spiders are the
same color as flowers. They
lie in ambush on flowers,
waiting for prey.

also hunters. They look somewhat like a
crab, and often run sideways as some crabs
do. Some crab spiders catch their prey by
running after it, but many kinds get their
food by lying in ambush.

Crab spiders are often white, yellow, or
pink. When they lie in wait on a flower that
is the same color, they are nearly invisible.
Any insect that comes onto the flower
usually won't see the spider—until it's too
late.

Spider giants!

The biggest spiders are a family of furry, black or brown creatures that live in warm parts of the world. In North America they are usually called tarantulas (tuh RAN chuh luhs). In other places they are known as hairy spiders or bird-eating spiders.

In South America, some of these spiders are large enough to cover a dinner plate! They are hunters. They creep over the ground or through the branches of trees, and leap on their prey. They usually hunt insects, but they also catch and eat birds, lizards, frogs, mice, and other large creatures!

Most people are afraid of such large spiders. A few kinds are dangerous, but most are not—their bite is no worse than a bee sting. Some kinds can be tamed, and even make good pets!

Water spiders

Some kinds of spiders like to live close to quiet ponds and swamps. And they "fish" for most of their food.

A fisher spider can run on top of the water. It can even stand on water without sinking in. It stands with its back legs on a water plant and its other legs on the water. When an insect, tadpole, or tiny fish swims close enough, the spider reaches down into the water and grabs it. The spider gives its catch a poisonous bite, then eats it.

In England, there are spiders that fish from rafts that they build! The "raft spider," as it is called, lives in marshy places where shallow water covers the ground. The spider makes its raft out of leaves and silk. Then it goes sailing along on the water, searching for prey. When it spies an insect, the spider runs across the water and grabs the creature. Then it carries its prey back to the raft to be eaten.

There's another spider found in England and parts of Europe that actually lives in the water. To make its house, the spider spins a silk sheet, underwater, among some plant leaves. Then it swims up to the top of the water to "collect" air. It collects air by lifting its back part up out of the water. Air is caught by hairs on the spider's body. When the spider swims back down, it

A water spider's house is a dome of silk filled with a bubble of air. As the air is used up, the spider brings more air bubbles from the surface of the water.

carries a bubble of air, wrapped around the back part of its body.

The spider swims under her silk sheet and brushes the bubble off against it. The air bubble tries to float up to the top of the water, of course. But it is held down by the silk sheet. Back and forth goes the spider, bringing air to the house. Soon, the silk sheet is so full of air pushing it up, that it looks like a silvery bell.

The spider spends most of its life in this house. Of course, as the spider breathes it uses up the air in the house. It has to go and get more from time to time.

When two of these water spiders mate, the male spider builds a smaller house close to the female's house. He connects the two houses with a tunnel of silk. The eggs are laid in the female's house and the babies hatch there.

jumping spider

A skillful jumper

A brightly colored little spider crouched on
a tree branch. Its two big eyes—and six
smaller ones—watched a fat fly. The fly sat
on the end of the branch, a good twelve
inches (30 centimeters) away. There seemed
no way for the spider to catch the fly. It was
too far away. If the spider dashed toward it,
the fly would simply zoom off.

Suddenly, the spider jumped. It sailed swiftly through the air—and landed right on the surprised fly's back! Soon, the spider was contentedly feasting.

Jumping spiders don't have long, powerful legs like a grasshopper or cricket. But they can make truly marvelous leaps. If you could jump as well as a jumping spider, you'd be able to leap more than two hundred feet (60 meters)! These spiders also have marvelous eyesight. They can see their prey a foot (30 cm) or more away. And they can judge the distance perfectly.

Jumping spiders are even able to catch flying insects in midair! As the spider leaps, it lets out a long thread of silk from its spinnerets. The end of the thread is attached to the place from which the spider jumped. This "lifeline" keeps the spider from falling. After catching its prey, the spider climbs back up the line and has dinner.

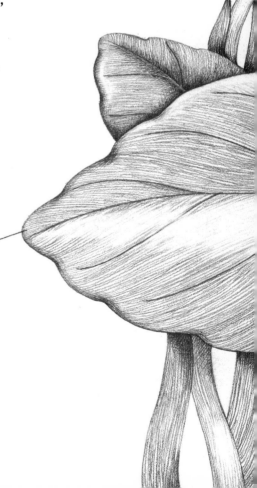

Dangerous spiders

Most spiders are harmless, and even rather helpless. They will almost always scurry out of your way unless forced to defend themselves. Although many spiders have a poisonous bite, the bite of most spiders won't hurt you. However, the bite of some of the large wolf spiders can be as painful as a bee sting. And the bite of a very few kinds of spiders can cause pain, sickness, and even death.

The black widow spider, which lives in North America, can be dangerous. It often makes its web in the corners of garages, barns, or sheds. The black widow is black with a red mark shaped like an hourglass on its underside.

The red-back spider, which lives in Australia, is related to the black widow. This spider is also dangerous. It is black, with a broad red stripe on its back.

Another dangerous North American spider is the brown recluse. It sometimes hides in closets, drawers, or under furniture. It is brown, with a black mark shaped like a violin on its back.

black widow spider

Flying spiders

The first few days in the life of most spiders are a time of great adventure. Soon after a spiderling breaks out of its egg sac, it climbs up a tall grass stem or to the top of a bush. Then, facing into the warm spring breeze, it lets out its silken threads.

The breeze catches the strands of thread and pulls the spiderling into the air! Up, up, and away it goes! The bits of thread are like a balloon, which is why this strange sight is called ballooning.

How far will the spiderling fly? If the breeze dies, the spiderling may go only a short distance. But it can take off again. By increasing the length of the threads, a spider can go higher. And by shortening the threads, it can come down.

Spiders have come down on ships as far as two hundred miles (320 kilometers) from land! And they have been found at a height of ten thousand feet (3,000 meters)!

Why do spiderlings journey through the air? This is nature's way of helping them survive. Hundreds of baby spiderlings come out of every egg sack. If they stayed where they hatched, there wouldn't be enough food for all. By soaring off into the sky, each spiderling has a chance to come down in a place where there are no other spiders.

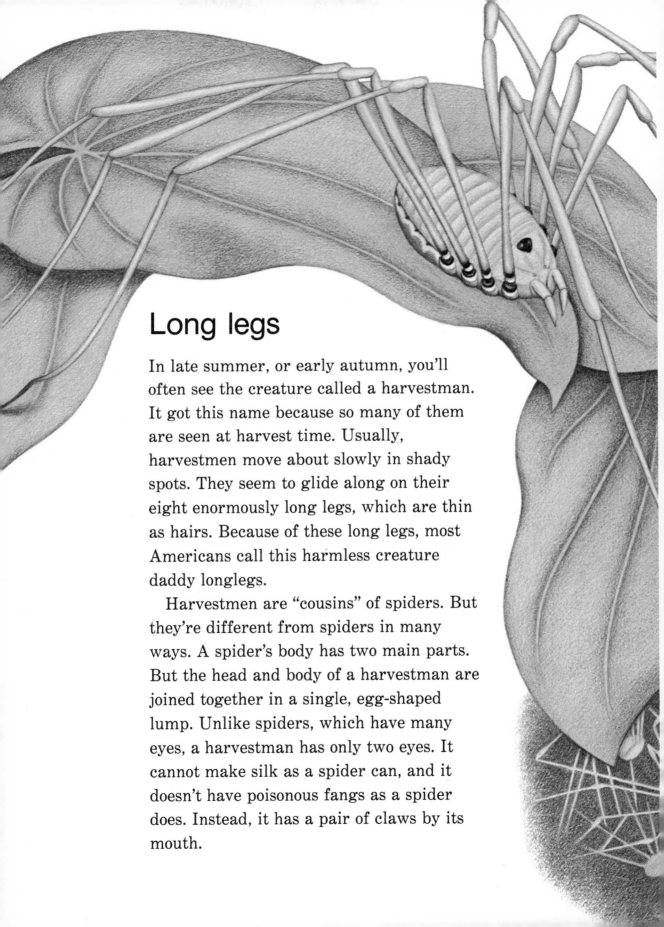

Long legs

In late summer, or early autumn, you'll
often see the creature called a harvestman.
It got this name because so many of them
are seen at harvest time. Usually,
harvestmen move about slowly in shady
spots. They seem to glide along on their
eight enormously long legs, which are thin
as hairs. Because of these long legs, most
Americans call this harmless creature
daddy longlegs.

Harvestmen are "cousins" of spiders. But
they're different from spiders in many
ways. A spider's body has two main parts.
But the head and body of a harvestman are
joined together in a single, egg-shaped
lump. Unlike spiders, which have many
eyes, a harvestman has only two eyes. It
cannot make silk as a spider can, and it
doesn't have poisonous fangs as a spider
does. Instead, it has a pair of claws by its
mouth.

Most kinds of harvestmen eat tiny insects that they tear to pieces with their claws. They'll also eat any large, dead insects they come across. Some kinds of harvestmen can break open snail shells with their strong claws. They then dig out the snail, bit by bit. And some kinds of harvestmen drink the juice of fruit by squeezing the fruit with their claws.

Harvestmen defend themselves against some enemies by squirting a bad smell out of openings in their body. And if a bird grabs a harvestman by one of its long legs, the leg comes off. It wiggles as if it were alive, and keeps the bird busy while the harvestman escapes.

Female harvestmen lay their eggs in the ground, under stones, or in cracks in tree bark. They lay their eggs in autumn. The babies hatch the following summer. They usually stay in hiding most of the summer, while they are growing up.

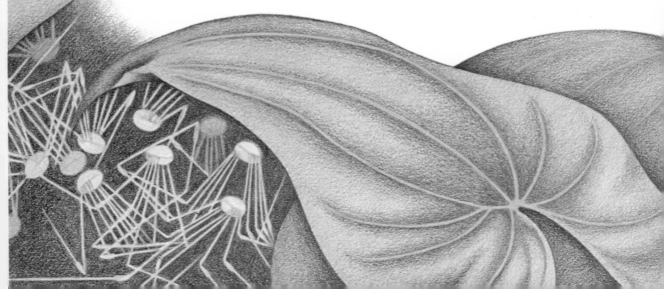

The tail-stinger

Scorpions live in the warm places, such as deserts. During the day, they usually hide in narrow spaces between rocks, or in shallow pits they dig beneath stones. At night, they come out to hunt. They scuttle about in search of beetles, cockroaches, and spiders.

scorpion eating a centipede

A scorpion kills its prey with the poisonous stinger on its tail. The scorpion curls its tail forward over its head and jabs the stinger into the prey.

Scorpions are eight-legged arachnids, like spiders and harvestmen. But unlike their "cousins," scorpions have a long, jointed tail with a sting at the end. By the mouth, there are two powerful "arms" with big, pinching claws. Scorpions have two large eyes and from four to ten small eyes.

A scorpion uses its claws to grab its prey. The victim is then pulled to the scorpion's sharp mouth parts and chewed up. If the insect or spider is large, and tries to fight, the scorpion kills it with a poisonous sting. The stinger is a sharp, curved spike at the end of the scorpion's tail. The scorpion curls its tail forward, over its head, and jabs the sting into its prey's body. The stings of some scorpions are dangerous to people.

Scorpions often eat other scorpions. So they live alone, except when two of them stay together for a while to mate. But after they have mated, the female usually kills the male and eats him!

Female scorpions do not lay eggs. The babies come out of their mother's body, a few at a time, over a period of several weeks. They climb up onto their mother's back and hang on as she carries them with her everywhere. If some of them fall off, the mother stops and searches for them until they climb back on. After a week or so, the young ones drop off and scamper away to start life on their own.

Other Tiny Creatures

millipede

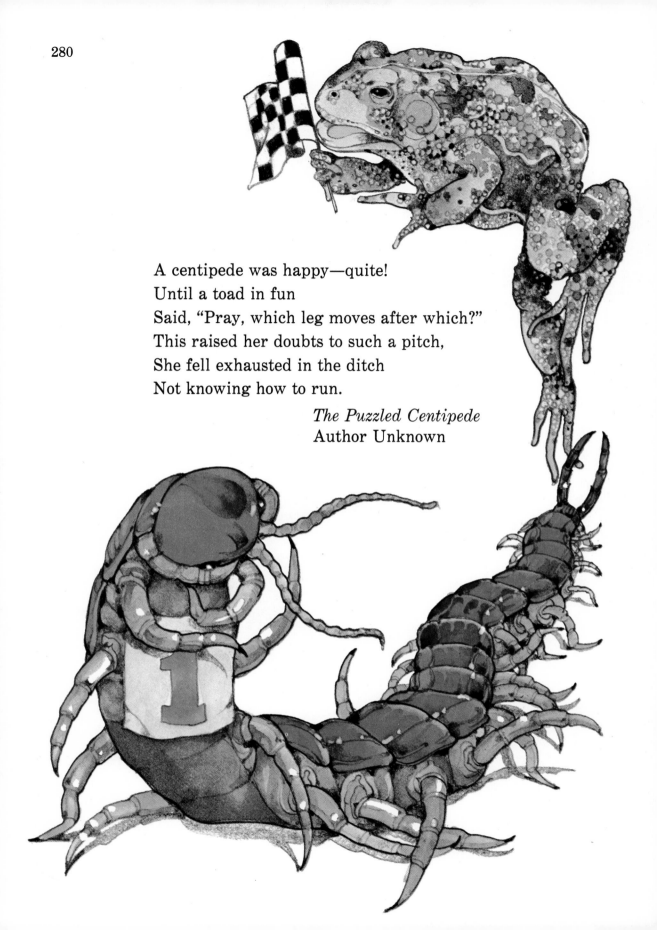

A centipede was happy—quite!
Until a toad in fun
Said, "Pray, which leg moves after which?"
This raised her doubts to such a pitch,
She fell exhausted in the ditch
Not knowing how to run.

The Puzzled Centipede
Author Unknown

"Hundred feet"

The little, wormlike animal lay in the darkness beneath a flat stone. It was the kind of animal called a slug. If it could have thought, the slug would probably have thought it was quite safe. What could get at it under the stone?

But another creature was also under the stone. It was a centipede (SEHN tuh peed), and it was hunting. With its many feet and long, flat body, it moved quickly and easily in the narrow space. Its feelers jerked and twitched. One of them touched the slug.

In an instant, the sharp fangs on the centipede's jaws stabbed into the slug's body. Poison squirted through the hollow fangs and the slug's life was over. The centipede began to chew.

There are many kinds of centipedes. All are fast, fierce hunters. They hunt in dark places, beneath stones, logs, and piles of leaves. They prey mostly on silverfish, cockroaches, worms, and slugs.

Most kinds of centipedes are small. But in the West Indies, there are very large centipedes. They often catch mice and lizards, as well as large insects.

A centipede's narrow body is divided into many sections. Each section has one pair of legs. The name *centipede* means "hundred feet." And some people call these creatures

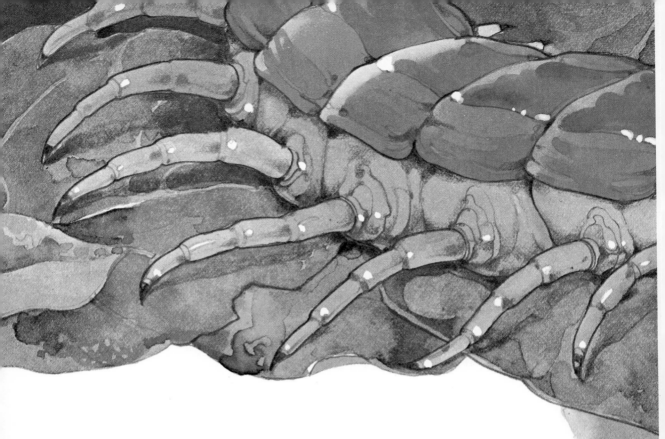

"hundred-legged worms." But no centipede has exactly one hundred legs. Most have about seventy legs. But some centipedes have only thirty, and others have more than three hundred!

Centipedes, like insects and spiders, hatch from eggs. Some kinds of baby centipedes look just like their parents. Others have only a few legs when they hatch. Each time they shed their skin, they gain more legs.

One kind of centipede likes to live and hunt in peoples' houses. Most people try to kill a centipede if they see one in the house. But they shouldn't. A house centipede is harmless. And it can be helpful. It will keep the house clean of roaches, flies, silverfish, and other creatures that are harmful.

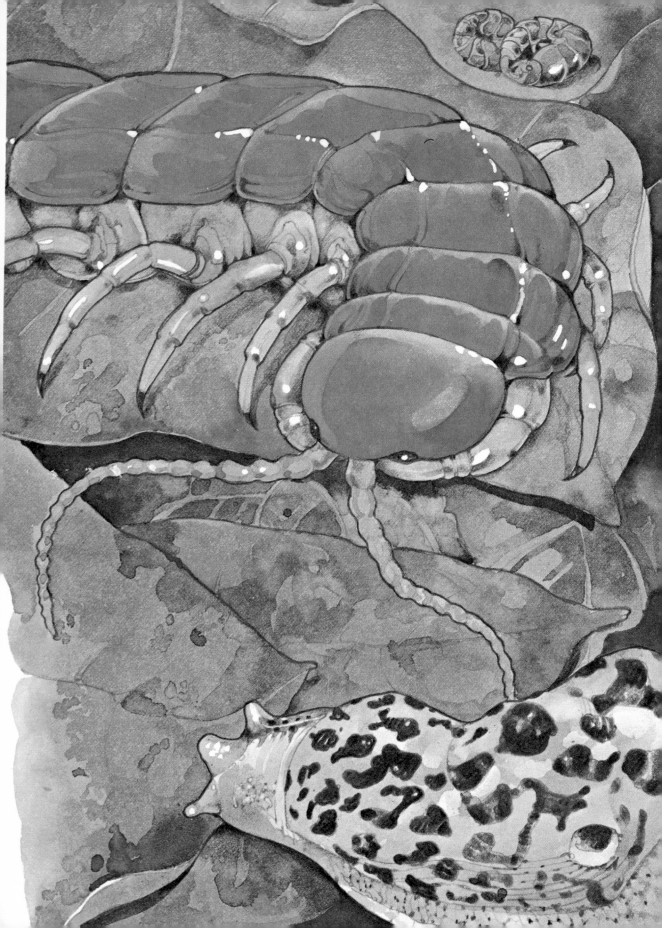

"Thousand feet"

Millipedes, like centipedes, usually live under logs, rocks, and piles of leaves. But their way of life is very different from that of a centipede. Millipedes crawl about very slowly. And they aren't hunters. They mostly eat bits of dead, rotting plants. Some also eat the roots of plants. This causes problems for gardeners and farmers.

Millipedes defend themselves with poison. They give off a liquid that has a stinging, burning, bitter taste. Birds or other animals that try to eat a millipede get a real taste shock. A millipede also has a hard shell, which protects it when it curls up in a circle.

Millipedes come from eggs. Some kinds of millipedes make a nest for their eggs. The

millipede

Millipedes are sometimes called "thousand-legged worms." But they really never have more than about 240 legs.

female builds a hollow dome out of dirt she mixes with liquid from her mouth. She lays from sixty to one hundred eggs through a hole in the top of the dome. Then she seals up the opening and goes on her way.

The young millipedes hatch in about twelve days. At first, they have only a few pairs of legs. As they get older, they add more legs.

The name *millipede* (MIHL uh peed) means "thousand feet." And some people do call millipedes "thousand-legged worms." But no millipede has this many legs. The greatest number of legs is about 240.

There are about eight thousand known kinds of millipedes. They live in all parts of the world. But there are probably many kinds scientists have not yet discovered.

Sow bugs

Lift up a flat stone that's lying on moist earth. Move a cardboard box that's been sitting in a damp basement. Peek under some wet leaves lying in a woods. Under any of these things you're almost sure to find some of the little oval-shaped creatures known as sow bugs or wood lice.

sow bugs

Sow bugs have gills, as many sea animals do. They live in damp places in order to keep water in their gills.

A sow bug looks fat, but it really has a thin, flat body. Its back is covered by a number of hard, curved shells. The shells overlap, so that the sow bug can bend. The sow bug's twelve, fourteen, or sixteen legs stick out from under the shells.

curled-up sow bugs

Sow bugs hide during the day. At night, they come out to eat bits of rotting plants. Sow bugs have to stay in damp places because they need moisture. Although they're land animals, they don't breathe air. They have gills that take oxygen out of water, just like many sea animals. So, they have to keep moisture in their gills to stay alive. Once a sow bug begins to dry up, it will die in about two hours.

Some kinds of sow bugs often lie curled upon their side, in a tight circle. This helps to keep the sow bug from drying up. And in this position, the sow bug is protected by the shells on its back. A curled-up sow bug looks very much like an old-fashioned pill. This is why these creatures are often called pill bugs.

A mother sow bug lays her eggs in a skin sack that grows on her body. The eggs hatch in the sack, and the babies stay there for a time. Finally, the sack tears open and the babies slip out, one at a time. After the babies are all out, the sack shrinks. When the mother sheds her skin, the sack goes with it.

Water bears

If you could shrink to the size of a pinpoint, you'd just be about as big as the strange creature called a water bear. Water bears are tiny, tiny many-legged animals. Seen with a powerful microscope, a water bear does look a bit like a fat, lumpy bear—but one with eight legs and lacy-looking armor on its back.

Some kinds of water bears live in ponds and mud puddles. Others lives on wet moss, in wet soil or sand, or among wet dead leaves on the ground.

A water bear has a mouth like a short tube, with a sharp horn on each side. Most water bears eat by poking holes in plants and sucking juice out of them. But a few kinds eat tiny worms and other very small creatures.

Quite often, the puddle, or other moist place where water bears live, dries up. Then the water bears dry up, too. They stop moving and eating. Their bodies fold up into hard, dry little bundles. They are as good as dead.

A water bear can stay this way for months and years. It may be picked up by the wind and carried for miles, like a bit of dust. But if it comes down in a wet place, or if rain falls where it is lying, an amazing thing happens. The water bear's hard, dry

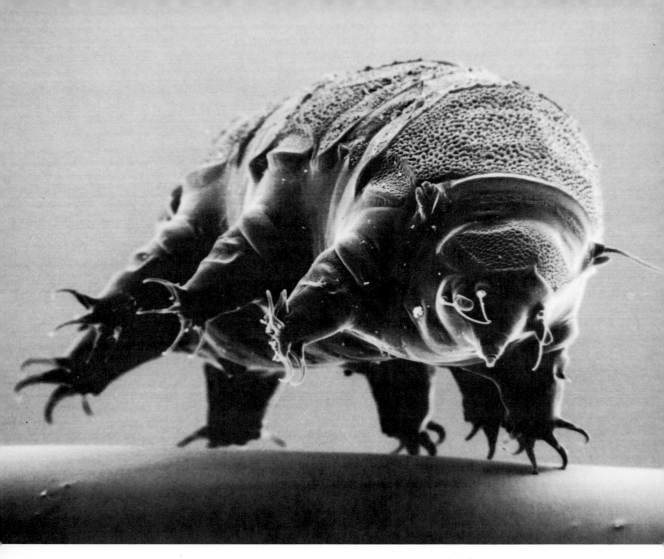

water bear

The eight-legged animal called a water bear is about the size of a pinpoint. This photograph was taken with a very powerful microscope.

body becomes soft and moist again. Soon, the little creature is ambling about in search of food as if nothing had happened! Some scientists once brought back to life some water bears that had been "dead" for more than a hundred years!

Water bears aren't related to insects, arachnids, centipedes, or millipedes. They are a strange group of eight-legged creatures that aren't quite like anything else on earth.

An "in-between" animal

It was night. A creature was hunting on a rotting log in a hot forest in Australia.

The creature had fourteen pairs of short, stubby legs, but it moved very slowly. The long, thick antennae on its head twitched and wiggled in a slow motion. It wasn't a fast hunter. But, it didn't have to be.

A fly buzzed down onto the log. It settled about a foot (30 centimeters) away from the hunter. That was close enough. From a bump on each side of its head, the hunter shot a spray of sticky slime. This landed on the surprised fly, which suddenly found itself stuck to the log. As the fly struggled to escape, the hunter moved slowly toward it. Sharp claws pierced the fly's body. The hunter began to eat.

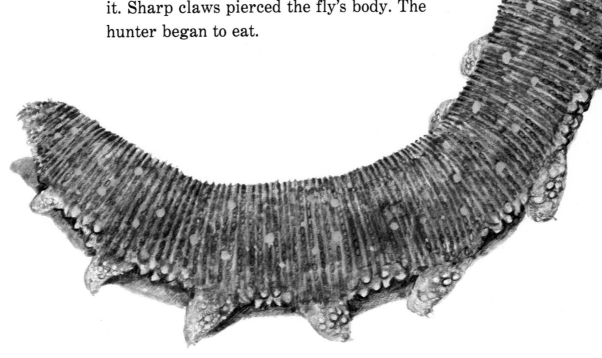

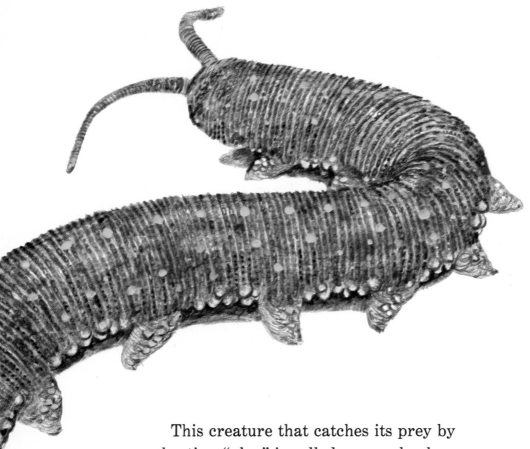

This creature that catches its prey by shooting "glue" is called an onychophoran (ah nuh KAHF uhr uhn). It's a very strange sort of animal. An onychophoran has a long, wormlike body and eyes and jaws like some kinds of worms. But it has antennae, as do most kinds of insects. It also has little claws on its feet, such as insects have. Its name, *onychophoran*, means "having claws."

There are about seventy different kinds of onychophorans. They live in Australia, Southeast Asia, and parts of South America and Africa. They live in rotting logs, under stones, and in piles of leaves. They come out at night to hunt flies, pill bugs, snails, worms, and other creatures.

Books to read

There are many fine books about the creatures of the insect world. The books listed here are only a sampling. The librarian at your school or public library will help you find these, or others just as good.

Ages 5 to 8

All Upon a Stone by Jean Craighead George (Crowell, 1971)
The story of the adventures of a mole cricket as it crawls upon a large stone in the woods.

Ants Are Fun by Mildred Myrick (Harper & Row, 1978)
Three boys set out to rebuild an ant colony, and learn a lot of interesting things about ants.

Aranea: A Story About a Spider by Jenny Wagner (Bradbury, 1978)
This little story tells of a spider that, each day, must spin a web she depends on for food.

Find the Hidden Insect by Joanna Cole and Jerome Wexler (Morrow, 1979)
Clear pictures show the ways that many kinds of insects hide by blending into the background.

Fireflies by Joan Ryder (Harper & Row, 1977)
An easy-to-follow presentation of the life cycle of these fascinating insects that are favorites of most children.

Green Darner: The Story of a Dragonfly by Robert McClung (Morrow, 1980)
The life of a dragonfly, as a nymph living in the watery world of a pond and as an adult hunter of the air.

The Honeybee by Paula Hogan (Raintree, 1979)
Clear pictures and easy-to-read text cover the life cycle of the honeybee and explain what the queen, workers, and drones do.

Insects Do the Strangest Things by Leonora Hornblow (Random House, 1968)
Interesting facts and pictures about ants, ladybugs, dragonflies, termites, and many other insects.

I Watch Flies by Gladys Conklin (Holiday House, 1977)
Easy text introduces young children to some of the common harmless and harmful flies of the world.

Ladybug by Robert McClung (Morrow, 1966)
The world and way of life of this helpful insect, another favorite of children, is covered in easy text and colorful pictures.

My Daddy Long-Legs by Judy Hawes (Crowell, 1972)
How to look for and study this creature, a relative of the spider.

Praying Mantis: The Garden Dinosaur by Gladys Conklin (Holiday House, 1978)
This book describes the life of the mantis and tells how to take care of a mantis as a pet.

When Insects Are Babies by Gladys Conklin (Holiday House, 1969)
The stages from egg to adult of sixteen different kinds of insects.

You Can Make an Insect Zoo by Roberta Hortense Roberts (Children's Press, 1974)
How to make insect cages and feed and care for many kinds of captive insects.

Ages 9 to 12

An Ant Is Born by Harald Doering
  (Sterling, 1964)
The birth, growth, and daily life of an
ant. Several kinds of ants are
discussed.

Bug Hunters by Ada and Frank
  Graham (Delacorte, 1978)
The story of the U.S. Department of
Agriculture's "war" against the
destructive cereal leaf beetle.
Interesting information about the
search for helpful insects to control
harmful ones, and about the danger to
the environment of chemical pesticides.

**Butterflies and Moths: How They
  Function** by Dorothy Hinshaw
  Patent (Holiday House, 1979)
The life, ecological role, and
relationship to humans of moths and
butterflies. The author is a zoologist.

Collecting Cocoons by Lois J. Hussey
  and Catherine Pessino
  (Crowell, 1953)
This book describes the life of a typical
moth and tells how to collect and care
for cocoons.

Deadly Ants by Seymour Simon
  (Four Winds, 1979)
The life and habits of the two most
dangerous ants—army ants and fire
ants—and safeguards against them.

Desert Hunter: The Spider Wasp
  by Barbara Williams (Harvey House,
  1975)
The life of a wasp that lives in the
desert and hunts spiders.

First You Catch a Fly by
  Ric Estrada (McCall, 1970)
A book of experiments and projects
involving flies. The only materials
needed can be found around the house.

Fully illustrated information is given
on capturing, raising, and studying
these insects that play a surprisingly
large part in our lives.

How Insects Communicate by
  Dorothy Hinshaw Patent (Holiday
  House, 1979)
This book gives interesting examples of
the many ways such insects as ants and
bees communicate with one another.

Insect Masquerades by Hilda Simon
  (Viking, 1968)
This illustrated book shows the ways
insects use camouflage and disguise to
protect themselves and to get food.

Insects by Jean Henri Fabre
  (Scribners, 1979)
Fabre, a schoolteacher, spent his life
studying insects and spiders. He
became a world-renowned expert. This
book tells about his life and describes
his experiments in his own words.

Keeping Insects as Pets
  by Ross and Pat Olney (Watts, 1978)
All the basic information a young
person needs in order to keep and care
for ants, mantises, crickets, moths,
butterflies, and spiders.

A Mosquito Is Born by William and
  Sara Jane White (Sterling, 1974)
Good photos and detailed text describe
the life cycle of a mosquito and the part
it has played in human history as a
disease carrier.

Paper Hornets by Ross E. Hutchins
  (Addison, 1973)
The life and activities of a colony of
hornets throughout a year.

The Bug Club Book by Gladys
  Conklin (Holiday House, 1966)
Ideas for starting a club to study and
collect insects.

New Words

Here are some of the words you have met in this book. Many of them may be new to you. All are useful words to know, and most have something to do with "bugs." Next to each word, you'll see how to say the word: **amphibian** (am FIHB ee uhn). The part in capital letters is said more loudly than the rest of the word. One or two sentences tell what the word means.

amphibian (am FIHB ee uhn)
An amphibian is an animal that lives in water and breathes with gills when it is young. Later, it usually develops lungs and is able to live on land. Frogs are amphibians. (For more information, see Volume 5, *About Animals*, pages 98-109.)

antenna (an TEHN uh)
An antenna is one of the two feelers that most insects and some other creatures have on their head. The plural is antennae (an TEHN ee).

arachnid (uh RAK nihd)
An arachnid is an eight-legged animal with a two-part body. Spiders and daddy longlegs are arachnids.

armadillo (ahr muh DIHL oh)
An armadillo is an animal that has a hard, bony shell. When attacked, it can roll itself into a ball to protect itself. (For more information, see Volume 5, *About Animals*, page 304.)

burrow (BUHR oh)
A burrow is a hole dug in the ground by an animal and used as a home.

chrysalis (KRIHS uh lihs)
A chrysalis is a hard shell, or case, that forms around a caterpillar when it starts to turn into a butterfly.

cocoon (kuh KOON)
A cocoon is a silk covering that many kinds of insect larvae spin around themselves when they are about to turn into adults.

colony (KAHL uh nee)
A group of animals or plants of the same kind, living together, is called a colony.

crustacean (kruhs TAY shun)
A crustacean is a kind of animal that has a shell-covered body and many legs. Crustaceans live mostly in water or damp places. Lobsters, crabs, and shrimp are crustaceans. (For more information, see Volume 5, *About Animals*, pages 116-117.)

digest (duh JEHST)
Digest means to change food in the body so that the body can use it for energy. (For more information, see Volume 14, *About Me*, pages 64-66.)

drone (drohn)
A drone is a male bee. Drones don't do any work and cannot sting. Their purpose is to mate with a queen, so that she will produce eggs.

fang (fang)
A fang is a long, pointed tooth. Dogs, wolves, and snakes have fangs.

fertilizer (FUR tuh ly zuhr)
Fertilizer is material that is added to soil to help plants grow.

fungus (FUHNG guhs)
A fungus is a plant that does not have leaves, flowers, or green coloring. A mushroom is a fungus. Two or more such plants are called fungi (FUHN jy). For more information, see Volume 6, *The Green Kingdom*, pages 130-131.)

gill (gihl)
A gill is a breathing organ that enables fish and many other water animals to take oxygen from water.

hive (hyv)
A hive is the name for a place where honeybees live and store their honey. It can be in a hollow tree or log, or it can be a box made by people.

honeycomb (HUHN ee kohm)
A honeycomb is a wax structure with six-sided compartments called cells.

Bees make a honeycomb out of wax that comes from their bodies. They use the cells to store honey, pollen, and eggs.

honeydew (HUHN ee doo)
Honeydew is the sweet liquid that tiny insects called aphids make by sucking juice from leaves. Honeydew drips from leaves in hot weather.

insect (IHN sehkt)
Any one of a group of small animals with six legs and a body that is divided into three parts. Most, but not all, have feelers and wings.

larva (LAHR vuh)
A larva is a young insect, from the time it leaves the egg until it becomes a **pupa**. A caterpillar is the larva of a butterfly or a moth.

lichen (LY kuhn)
Lichen is a plant that grows on rocks and trees. It is actually two plants, fungi and algae, growing together. (For more information, see Volume 6, *The Green Kingdom*, page 101.)

mammal (MAM uhl)
A mammal is any one of a group of warm-blooded animals that is fed milk from the mother's body, has some hair on its body, and has a skeleton. Dogs, cats, whales, and people are mammals.

migrate (MY grayt)
Some insects and birds migrate, or go from one part of the world to another when the seasons change.

mobile (MOH buhl)
Mobile means able to move.

molt (mohlt)
To molt means to shed old skin, hair, feathers, or other things that grow on the body to make room for new growth. Insects, spiders, snakes, and many other creatures shed their entire outer skin when they molt.

monarch (MAHN uhrk)
A monarch is a ruler, such as a king or queen.

nectar (NEHK tuhr)
Nectar is a sweet liquid that is made by many kinds of flowers. Butterflies and many other insects live on nectar. Bees make it into honey.

nymph (nihmf)
A nymph is the young form, or **larva**, of an insect that changes directly to the adult stage and then lives on land. It looks like the adult but has no wings or only small wings.

oblong (AHB lawng)
An oblong is a shape that is longer than it is wide. A loaf of bread is usually oblong.

oval (OH vuhl)
Oval means egg-shaped.

plague (playg)
A plague is a dangerous disease that spreads very quickly and causes a great many deaths.

pollen (PAHL uhn)
Pollen is a yellowish powder that is made in the parts of a flower called the anthers. When pollen from one flower gets into another flower of the same kind, a seed is formed. (For more information, see Volume 6, *The Green Kingdom*, page 38.)

prey (pray)
Prey is any animal that is hunted or chased by another animal.

pupa (pyoo puh)
A pupa is a stage in the development of many kinds of insects. The **larva** changes into a pupa, which, in turn, develops into an adult.

reptile (REHP tuhl)
A reptile is a scaly, cold-blooded, air-breathing animal with a skeleton. Most reptiles hatch from eggs. Lizards, snakes, and alligators are reptiles. (For more information, see Volume 5, *About Animals*, pages 82-97.)

survive (suhr VYV)
Survive means to stay alive, to keep from being killed.

Illustration acknowledgments

The publishers of *Childcraft* gratefully acknowledge the courtesy of the following photographers, agencies, and organizations for illustrations in this volume. When all the illustrations for a sequence of pages are from a single source, the inclusive page numbers are given. In all other instances, the page numbers refer to facing pages, which are considered as a single unit or spread. All illustrations are the exclusive property of the publishers of *Childcraft* unless names are marked with an asterisk (*).

Cover: Aristocrat and Standard binding—Edward S. Ross*
Heritage binding—Richard Hook; Edward S. Ross*;
Jean Helmer; Edward S. Ross*; Jerry Pinkney;
Edward S. Ross*
1: Roberta Polfus
2–9: Edward S. Ross*
10–11: Gwen Connelly
12–13: Hana Sawyer; Edward S. Ross*
14–15: Jeff March Nature Photography*; Patricia Wynne
16–17: Richard Hook; Hana Sawyer
18–19: Edward S. Ross*
20–21: Edward S. Ross*; Oxford Scientific Films*
22–23: Richard Hook
24–25: Grant Heilman*; Gwen Connelly
26–27: Patricia Wynne; Edward S. Ross*
28–29: Edward S. Ross*; ©William E. Ferguson*; David Scharf from Peter Arnold, Inc.*
30–31: Richard Hook
32–33: Richard Hook; Edward S. Ross*
34–35: Gwen Connelly
36–37: Edward S. Ross*
38–39: Patricia Wynne; Thomas Eisner (Cornell University)*
40–41: Richard Hook
42–43: Robert T. Smith, Ardea Photographics*
44–45: Edward S. Ross*
46–47: Patricia Wynne; Edward S. Ross*
48–49: Edward S. Ross*
50–51: Jerry Pinkney
52–53: Edward S. Ross*
54–59: Jerry Pinkney
60–63: Edward S. Ross*
64–65: Jerry Pinkney
66–67: Richard Hook; Edward S. Ross*
68–71: Richard Hook
72–73: Edward S. Ross*
74–77: Richard Hook
78–79: Richard Hook; Edward S. Ross*
80–81: Richard Hook
82–83: Edward S. Ross*; Richard Hook
84–85: Edward S. Ross*
86–91: Pamela Baldwin Ford
92–93: Edward S. Ross*; Jane Burton, Bruce Coleman Ltd.*
94–95: Pamela Baldwin Ford
96–97: Edward S. Ross*
98–99: Edward S. Ross*; Jean Helmer
100–101: Jean Helmer
102–103: Edward S. Ross*
104–105: James P. Rowan*
106–107: Gwen Connelly
108–109: Edward S. Ross*; Gwen Connelly
110–111: Gwen Connelly
112–113: Edward S. Ross*
114–115: Edward S. Ross*; Hana Sawyer
116–117: Edward S. Ross*; Gwen Connelly
118–119: Edward S. Ross*; Hana Sawyer
120–121: ©Kjell B. Sandved*
122–127: Patricia Wynne
128–129: Edward S. Ross*
130–131: Edward S. Ross*; Hana Sawyer
132–133: Mark Johnson*
134–141: Jerry Pinkney
142–143: Edward S. Ross*

144–145: Patricia Wynne
146–147: Edward S. Ross*
148–149: Jean Helmer
150–151: Norman Weaver
152–155: Edward S. Ross*
156–157: Jean Helmer
158–159: Patricia Wynne
160–165: Edward S. Ross*
166–167: James P. Rowan*
168–175: Gwen Connelly
176–177: Gwen Connelly; Edward S. Ross*
178–179: Walter Linsenmaier
180–181: Edward S. Ross*
182–185: Roberta Polfus
186–187: Roberta Polfus; Susan Stamato
188–189: Edward S. Ross*
190–191: Edward S. Ross*; Susan Stamato
192–193: Edward S. Ross*
194–195: Gwen Connelly
196–197: Richard Hook
198–199: Edward S. Ross*
200–201: Patricia Wynne
202–203: Patricia Wynne; Edward S. Ross*
204–207: Edward S. Ross*
208–209: Richard Hook
210–211: Edward S. Ross*
212–213: Patricia Wynne
214–217: Edward S. Ross*
218–219: Gwen Connelly
220–223: Roberta Polfus
224–225: Edward S. Ross*
226–227: Hana Sawyer
228–229: Patricia Wynne; Edward S. Ross*
230–231: Edward S. Ross*; Patricia Wynne
232–233: Patricia Wynne
234–235: Oxford Scientific Films*
236–237: Jerry Pinkney
238–239: Richard Hook
240–241: Richard Hook; Edward S. Ross*
242–243: Edward S. Ross*
244–245: ©William E. Ferguson*
246–247: Gwen Connelly
248–249: Roberta Polfus; John H. Gerard, DPI*
250–251: J. A. L. Cooke, Oxford Scientific Films*; E. R. Degginger*
252–253: Mark Stowe*; Ann Moreton*; Roberta Polfus
254–255: Jean Helmer
256–257: Roberta Polfus
258–259: Oxford Scientific Films*; Jean Helmer
260–261: Jack J. Kunz
262–263: Edward S. Ross*
264–265: Edward S. Ross*; Roberta Polfus
266–267: Jean Helmer
268–269: Oxford Scientific Films*
270–271: Oxford Scientific Films*; Roberta Polfus
272–273: Edward S. Ross*; Jean Helmer
274–275: Roberta Polfus
276–279: Edward S. Ross*
280–283: Jerry Pinkney
284–285: Edward S. Ross
286–287: Edward S. Ross; Richard Hook
288–289: Robert O. Schuster, University of California, Davis*
290–291: Richard Hook

Index

This index is an alphabetical list of the important things covered in both words and pictures in this book. The index shows you what page or pages each thing is on. For example, if you want to find out what the book tells about a particular subject, such as the bumblebee, look under bumblebee. You will find a group of words, called an entry, like this: **bumblebee,** 177, *with picture.* This entry tells you that you can read about the bumblebee on page 177. The words *with picture* tell you that there is a picture of a bumblebee on this page, too. Sometimes, the book only tells you about a thing and does not show a picture. Then the words *with picture* will not be in the entry. It will look like this: **leafhopper,** 204. Sometimes, there is only a picture of a thing in the book. Then the word *picture* will appear before the page number, like this: **carpenter ant,** picture, 132.

Cyclo-teacher® The easy-to-use learning system

Features hundreds of cycles from seven valuable learning areas

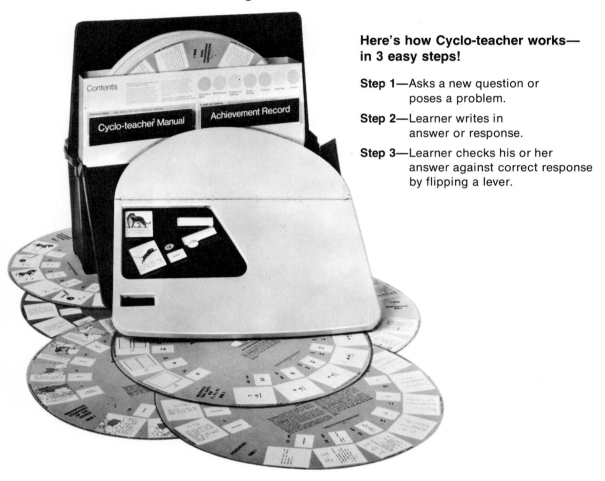

Here's how Cyclo-teacher works— in 3 easy steps!

Step 1—Asks a new question or poses a problem.

Step 2—Learner writes in answer or response.

Step 3—Learner checks his or her answer against correct response by flipping a lever.

Cyclo-teacher—the remarkable learning system based on the techniques of programmed instruction—comes right into your home to help stimulate and accelerate the learning of basic skills, concepts, and information. Housed in a specially designed file box are the Cyclo-teacher machine, Study Wheels, Answer Wheels, a Manual, a Contents and Instruction Card, and Achievement Record sheets.

Your child will find Cyclo-teacher to be a new and fascinating way to learn—much like playing a game. Only, Cyclo-teacher is much more than a game—it teaches new things

. . . reinforces learning . . . and challenges a youngster to go beyond!

Features hundreds of Study Cycles to meet the individual needs of students—your entire family—just as the *Childcraft Annual* is a valuable learning aid. And, best of all, lets you track your own progress—advance at your own pace! Cyclo-teacher is available by writing us at the address below:

The Childcraft Annual
Post Office Box 3822
Chicago, IL 60654

These beautiful bookstands—

specially designed to hold your entire program, including *Childcraft Annuals*.

Height: 26-3/8"
with 4" legs.
Width: 28-3/4"
Depth: 8-3/16"

Height: 8-3/4"
Width: 14-1/2"
Depth: 8"

Most parents like having a convenient place to house their *Childcraft Annuals* and their *Childcraft* library. A beautiful floor-model bookstand—constructed of solid hardwood—is available in either walnut or fruitwood finish.

You might prefer the attractive hardwood table racks, also available in either walnut or fruitwood finish. Let us know by writing us at the following address:

The Childcraft Annual
Post Office Box 3822
Chicago, IL 60654

moth

The
Bug
Book